PRAISE FOR *THE 4 JOBS CLUB*

"With its straightforward format and practical advice, *The 4 Jobs Club* isn't just another self-help book—it's a woman's go-to resource for navigating the complexities of modern life with ease. Whether you're climbing the career ladder or just trying to keep it all together, this book provides the support and solutions you need to succeed in your career while maintaining all the other responsibilities life throws at you. A practical resource for all ages and stages."

—Maryam Banikarim, Managing Director, Fortune: Most Powerful Women & Brainstorm Tech

"Kathryn highlights how important it is for women in senior-level roles to lead by example. We all must be vulnerable and transparent in our leadership so that other women can show up as their true selves and feel empowered as we navigate our roles as parents, partners, and professionals.

—Eve Rodsky, *New York Times* best selling author, *Fair Play*

"Kathryn Sollmann sheds light on the incredible balancing act many women face today. This book is a must-read for women determined to excel professionally while managing the demands of family and home."

—Subha V. Barry, President, Seramount

"A transformative read for anyone caught in the hustle and bustle of a career. *The 4 Jobs Club* offers a wealth of practical advice and insightful reflections that will help you find balance and maintain your sanity. It's a roadmap to a more harmonious and productive life."

—Isabelle Bajeux-Besnainou, Dean and Richard P. Simmons Professor of Finance, Tepper School of Business at Carnegie Mellon University

"As a working mom, and the author of seven books on leadership, I know first-hand the challenges of holding down more than one full-time job. In fact, I wrote my most recent book in the evenings, because that was the only time no one was asking me for food! The timeless tips in *The 4 Jobs Club* would have made my journey a lot less stressful. A must-read book for the women *and* men in your life!"

—Roberta Matuson, author, *Suddenly in Charge: Managing Up, Managing Down, Succeeding All Around*

"A must read for every woman trying to successfully navigate a thriving career and a vibrant home life! Kathryn offers a refreshing and much-needed look into juggling work and life as a woman in the modern world. *The 4 Jobs Club* gives real-life examples providing encouragement and inspiration to let go of guilt while working toward financial security, happiness and well-being."

—Kristel Bauer, Founder of Live Greatly, author, *Work/Life Tango*

The 4 Jobs Club

How Smart Women Care for It All: Kids, Aging
Parents, Home and Career

Over 200 Tips from 50 C-Suite Women

KATHRYN SOLLMANN

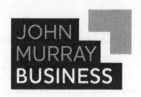

First Published by John Murray Business in 2025
An imprint of John Murray Press

A Hachette UK company

29 28 27 26 25   4 5 6 7 8 9 10

A CIP catalogue record for this title is available from the British Library

Library of Congress Control Number: 2024939374

ISBN 9781399818551
eBook ISBN 9781399818568

Printed and bound in Great Britain by Clays Ltd, Elcograf S.p.A.

John Murray Press policy is to use papers that are natural, renewable and recyclable products and made from wood grown in sustainable forests. The logging and manufacturing processes are expected to conform to the environmental regulations of the country of origin.

John Murray Press Ltd
Carmelite House
50 Victoria Embankment
London EC4Y 0DZ
Tel: 020 3122 6000

John Murray Business
123 South Broad Street
Ste 2750
Philadelphia, PA 19109

John Murray Press, part of Hodder & Stoughton Limited
An Hachette UK company

The authorised representative in the EEA is Hachette Ireland, 8 Castlecourt Centre, Dublin 15, D15 XTP3, Ireland (email: info@hbgi.ie)

For my daughters, Caroline and Gracyn,
who inspire me to help women find the work that fits their lives

CONTENTS

INTRODUCTION

Grocery shopping.

Cooking.

Cleaning.

Work projects.

Laundry.

Doctor appointments.

Caring for elderly parents.

Finding childcare.

Household repairs.

School projects.

Carpooling.

Birthday parties.

Yet another dinner.

The typical American woman is aspiring to be in what I call *THE 4 JOBS CLUB*, a comfortable place where you can actually manage all the tasks of four big jobs—a professional one, plus caring for children, aging parents, and households.

There is never enough time in a week, let alone a day. Many women reach the conclusion that something's gotta give—and too often the professional job seems the most expendable. In my career coaching practice, women pulled in four high-voltage directions tell me they need to leave the workforce for "a couple of years to get things in order."

Only 57.6 percent[1] of women were in the workforce in early 2024, supporting the fact that at some point 49 percent[2] of women step out for an extended period (usually two years beyond their maternity leave allowance).

My anecdotal data shows a much longer hiatus—information I've gathered after coaching hundreds of professional women since 2002. I see women staying out an average of 12 years, especially when their partners are at a more senior level. That's a whopping 144 paychecks not earned, saved, or invested. It's a big hit to a woman's long-term financial security, and a big hole in resumes when most women, inevitably, want to return.

But not all women take a hiatus and stall their careers. A small but slowly increasing number of women stay in and reach the C-suite. An S&P Global Market Intelligence study predicts, in fact, that women and men will have the same number of senior leadership roles by 2030.[3]

How do these women manage to fight their way through corporate gender barriers while at the same time managing 4 Jobs?

Cynics say that women scaling the corporate pyramid surely must 1) favor work over life, 2) have Mr. Mom husbands, 3) employ hot and cold running help, 4) never see their children, and 5) have a stress-busting masseuse at their beck and call.

Well, as to #2, some C-suite women do have husbands or partners who willingly traded professional jobs for caregiving, but it is by no means the norm. In my conversations with 50 prominent women who are chiefs of many corporate disciplines, I learned that they have two-income households pretty much like yours and mine.

To be fair, women who have the highest corporate earnings can certainly afford to outsource many household and caregiving responsibilities. But most saw the value in paying for as much help as they could afford—essentially investing in their careers—even when they were much lower in the ranks. They did so when outsourcing took a big chunk out of their on-the-way-up-the-ladder pay.

In pre-pandemic days, these C-suite women did a lot of traveling across the United States and abroad. It's a misperception, though, that they did not prioritize and maximize family time. They indeed continue to find ways to spend special time with their children, create family traditions, and stay involved at their kids' schools.

When it comes to self-care, the women I interviewed did not appear to be jetting off regularly to the trendiest spas. They go for walks and runs, visit museums, read books, and do the simple things we all do to take a break. The difference is that these women take a business approach to self-care—scheduling it, making it routine, and not apologizing for any time off they need.

The bottom line is that these C-suite women made non-life-shattering trade-offs, practiced anti-perfection, found shortcuts, asked for and paid for a reasonable amount of help, and found systems for household equity with their life partners. You will see that nothing they did was rocket science, over-the-top expensive, or detrimental to the health and well-being of their extended families.

I asked each woman how they managed to reach the C-suite with the competing demands of work and family. As a group they gave me more than 200 simple tips that helped them persevere and keep moving to the top. They asked for the flexibility they needed, focused on building a portfolio of skills, slowed down a bit if they had to, and reached for promotions when *they* felt the time was right.

It's great that these women reached the C-suite, but I'm not suggesting it's the path you need to take. As I made clear in my book *Ambition Redefined*,[4] the C-suite does not need to be every woman's goal. Some kind of ongoing work that fits your life, however, is definitely a wise approach. It's hard to argue with the fact that life takes many unexpected turns. Women need to always be able to support themselves and their families.

This book retires the battle-weary question "Can women have it all?" That emotionally charged question provokes self-criticism, plunging women into a negative place where they too often conclude they don't have the chops to do all 4 Jobs on their own. Instead, this book answers a more productive question that inspires collaboration and helps women reach long-term financial security: "How can smart women help other smart women *care for it all*?"

Whether you're managing a multimillion-dollar division or contributing to a small team, blending work and life for several decades takes creativity, organization, cutting yourself slack, exploring strategies, and asking for help. The relatively easy but powerful tips in this book are from women who have done that, managing four big jobs at every life stage and career level.

You can, too.

Join the club! Capitalizing on the wisdom of the 50 professional women who contributed to this book, you can stay in the workforce and be the professional, mother, daughter, and life partner you want to be.

Kathryn Sollmann
Wilton, Connecticut

CONTRIBUTORS

— Christine DeBiase, *Chief Legal Officer, General Counsel*
ALLSTATE

— Stephanie Richard, *Chief Audit Executive*
ALLY FINANCIAL

— Dana White, *Senior Managing Director*
Global Strategic Advisory Practice
ANKURA CONSULTING GROUP
Former Chief Communications Officer
HYUNDAI MOTOR NORTH AMERICA

— Mindy Simon, *Global Chief Operating Officer*
AON

— Julie Rosen, *President*
BATH & BODY WORKS

— Gregg Renfrew, *Entrepreneur*
Founder & Chief Executive Officer
BEAUTYCOUNTER

— Kimberly Paige, *Chief Marketing Officer*
BET NETWORKS

— Tonit Calaway, *Executive Vice President, Chief Administrative Officer,*
General Counsel and Secretary
BORGWARNER

— Chandra Dhandapani, *Former Chief Executive Officer*
CBRE | GLOBAL WORKPLACE SOLUTIONS

— Jordana Kammerud, *Chief Human Resources Officer*
CORNING INCORPORATED

— Mary K.W. Jones, *Former Senior Vice President, General Counsel and Worldwide Public Affairs*
DEERE & COMPANY

— Janet Foutty, *Former US Board Chair*
Former Chief Executive Officer, Deloitte Consulting LLP
DELOITTE

— Jonita Wilson, *Chief Diversity and Social Impact Officer*
DISCOVER FINANCIAL SERVICES

— Penny Pennington, *Managing Partner*
EDWARD JONES

— Anne White, *President, Lilly Neuroscience*
ELI LILLY

— Jenny Johnson, *President and Chief Executive Officer*
FRANKLIN TEMPLETON

— Marie Myers, *Executive Vice President and Chief Financial Officer*
HEWLETT PACKARD ENTERPRISE

— Jacinth Smiley, *Executive Vice President and Chief Financial Officer*
HORMEL FOODS

— Ana Maria Chadwick
Executive Vice President, Chief Financial Officer and Treasurer
INSULET
Former Chief Financial Officer
PITNEY BOWES

— Sharon Ryan, *Former Senior Vice President and General Counsel*
INTERNATIONAL PAPER

— Jill Penrose, *Chief People and Company Services Officer*
THE J.M. SMUCKER CO.

— Jennifer Piepszak, *Co-Chief Executive Officer,*
Commercial and Investment Bank
JPMORGANCHASE

— Dana Rosenfeld, *Firm Managing Partner*
KELLEY DRYE & WARREN LLP

— Jill Timm, *Chief Financial Officer*
KOHL'S

— Raj Seshadri, *Chief Commercial Payments Officer*
MASTERCARD

— Jacky Wright, *Chief Technology and Platform Officer*
MCKINSEY & COMPANY

— Martine Ferland, *Former President and Chief Executive Officer*
MERCER
Former Vice Chair
MARSH MCLENNAN

— Liz Mazzotta, *Chief Administrative Officer*
MUTUAL OF OMAHA

— Amy Shore, *Executive Vice President and*
Chief Customer Officer
NATIONWIDE

— Kris Malkoski, *Segment Chief Executive Officer,*
Learning & Development
NEWELL BRANDS

— Aditi Javeri Gokhale, *Chief Strategy Officer, President of Retail*
Investments and Head of Institutional Investments
NORTHWESTERN MUTUAL

— Monisha Dabek, *Chief Commercial Officer & General Manager USA*
OCEAN SPRAY

— Suzanne Powers, *Founder CEO*
POWERS CREATIVITY
Former Global Chief Product Officer
MCCANN WORLDGROUP
Former Chair
FUTUREBRAND

— Anne Foulkes, *Senior Vice President and General Counsel*
PPG

— Smita Pillai, *Chief Diversity, Equity and Inclusion Officer*
REGENERON PHARMACEUTICALS

— Karen Jones, *Chief Marketing Officer*
RYDER SYSTEM, INC.

— Linda Rutherford, *Chief Administration Officer*
SOUTHWEST AIRLINES

— Shannon Lapierre, *Former Chief Communications Officer*
STANLEY BLACK & DECKER

— Marie Robinson, *Former Chief Supply Chain Officer*
SYSCO

— Patricia L. Lewis, *Executive Vice President and
Chief Sustainability Officer*
UNITEDHEALTH GROUP

— Martha Leiper, *Chief Investment Officer*
UNUM GROUP

— Gunjan Kedia, *President*
U.S. BANCORP

— Jessica Graziano, *Chief Financial Officer*
U.S. STEEL

— Joy Corso, *Chief Marketing Officer and
Head of Integration*
VONAGE

— Christine Hurtsellers, *Former Chief Executive Officer,
Voya Investment Management*
VOYA FINANCIAL

— Nora Zimmett, *President, News and Original Series*
WEATHER GROUP

— Mary Mack, *Former Chief Executive Officer, Consumer and Small Business Banking*
WELLS FARGO

— Denise Merle, *Chief Administrative Officer*
WEYERHAEUSER

— Sharon Callahan-Miller, *Executive Coach*
WHAT'S POSSIBLE, INC.
Former Chief Client Officer
OMNICOM HEALTH GROUP
Former Chief Executive Officer
CDM NEW YORK

CONTRIBUTOR BIOGRAPHIES

Tonit Calaway
Executive Vice President, Chief Administrative Officer,
General Counsel and Secretary
BorgWarner

Raising her children with a sense of adventure and a love for the theater, Tonit, 56, may have had an inkling early on that both her children would head to the stage. From their home in Wisconsin, she often took them on international trips and to New York City to see Broadway plays. Now her 26-year-old daughter is pursuing an acting career, and she has produced an off-Broadway play. Her son, who is 21, is also an actor and working toward a degree in Art History at Yale.

A high-energy person who can operate at peak efficiency with as little as one hour of sleep, Tonit is go-go-go all day. She cares for herself both mentally and physically by exercising each morning with a personal trainer—running, lifting weights, and mixing up cardio and high-intensity workouts.

Because both Tonit and her husband have very demanding jobs (he is a judge for the Milwaukee County Circuit Court), outsourcing for extra household help has always been part of Tonit's self-care routine. Even in her early career she had someone help her clean the house—and as her income rose, she hired a housekeeper for additional days. Despite this help, there is still plenty to take care of in the household, and Tonit shares responsibilities pretty evenly with her husband.

Sharon Callahan-Miller
Executive Coach, What's Possible, Inc.
Former Chief Client Officer, Omnicom Health Group
Former Chief Executive Officer, CDM New York

At 62, Sharon is on her second round of parenting. After raising two boys on her own for 19 years, she got married six years ago. Now she and her wife have three-year-old twins, Maisy and Miles, along with Sharon's sons—Henry, 28, and Ben, 23.

Sharon has worked nonstop since college, and as an often single parent she had a part-time housekeeper/nanny to care for her boys after school. With a busy career that included frequent business travel, she also hired a housecleaner. Now she finds it easier to run a household with two parents. Her toddlers are in daycare, and she shares responsibilities with her wife, who also works full time and needs to be away one night a week for her work. Whenever it makes sense, the couple shares responsibilities fifty-fifty, but more often one accommodates the other's busy schedule at the high end of the ratio (eighty-twenty).

As Henry and Ben were growing up, they were always involved in sports, and Sharon attended their games as much as possible. She and her sons were avid Yankees and Knicks fans, and they often went to games as a family. Following Ben's graduation from Trinity College in Hartford, Connecticut, where he was captain of the basketball team, he is continuing to play basketball as he works toward his Master's in Public Administration at Binghamton University. His brother has taken a different path in television and film production and as a school paraprofessional.

Through the years, Sharon has experienced multigenerational caregiving. When she was in a senior management role, her mother died suddenly of an aortic embolism. She then was involved in her father's care when he lived in a nursing home with Alzheimer's for five years.

With Sharon's reinvention from corporate CEO to executive coach—and two toddlers at home in Massachusetts—her life is as busy as ever. Her outlet is yoga, which she fits in whenever she can.

Ana Maria Chadwick
Executive Vice President, Chief Financial Officer and Treasurer
Insulet
Former Chief Financial Officer
Pitney Bowes

At one time, Ana and her husband of 28 years both worked at GE. He then left to be the chief financial officer of several private equity companies, a work arrangement they thought was healthier than being at the same company.

Ana experienced progressively growing divisional CFO responsibilities at GE Capital until her fourth maternity leave. Upon return, she was given a lateral/ lower-tier assignment as a divisional Controller. She made the most of it for a year, then continued her upward trajectory, culminating as President and CEO, Global Legacy Solutions.

Following a recent Chief Financial Officer post at Pitney Bowes, Ana, 52, moved to Insulet, a company that develops insulin management systems. She juggles her career with four children—ranging from age nine to 23. She has a son who graduated from college with a degree in Computer Engineering and a daughter in college studying Communications and Public Relations. Another son and daughter are still at home in Connecticut.

With both her parents and in-laws in Puerto Rico, Chile, and Argentina, Ana has not been able to rely on grandparents for help with childcare. A live-in nanny has always cared for her young children, and this arrangement has allowed both Ana and her husband to pursue demanding careers.

Though Ana's weekday schedule is jam-packed, she makes time to prepare a nice breakfast for her two younger children before she leaves for work. Aside from occasional golf, her workout schedule includes kickboxing twice a week in the evenings, and she goes out with her husband every Friday night.

Joy Corso
Chief Marketing Officer and Head of Integration
Vonage

Up at about 5:00 a.m. each day, Joy, 54, is off and running. First, she scans emails and the news and triages anything important. She then gets a workout in and tries to be online by 7:00 a.m. After work she catches up with her family, does a final check of emails, looks at the news, and ends her night feeling ready for the next day.

A native New Englander, Joy and her family moved to Texas in 2011 for a career opportunity. Wherever Joy and her husband of 32 years have lived, they've split household responsibilities equitably.

Their daughters, now 18 and 19, were always very active in a variety of sports and extracurricular activities, which kept every weekend very busy. When the girls were young, they had a live-out nanny and the occasional help of Joy's dad.

As a family, they've traveled to many countries to build an appreciation for other cultures, and they've enjoyed being community volunteers.

Monisha Dabek
Chief Commercial Officer & General Manager USA
Ocean Spray

At age 45, Monisha is caring for two young children—an eight-year-old son and a five-year-old daughter—alongside a C-suite career.

Her husband of 18 years also has a demanding career as Senior Vice President of Operations at a government consulting/business process outsourcing company. With both parents at work, the family had a nanny until each child reached two years old, and then shifted to a childcare center. They now have part-time babysitting help after school.

Monisha's parents are within driving distance of their Massachusetts home, and they help with the children on weekends and when she has a long work trip. Her mother-in-law battled cancer for several years before she passed away. At the time, Monisha was at the Vice President/

Senior Vice President levels, and she and her husband had to find a careful balance of managing their careers while also prioritizing time with family.

Professional house cleaning is something Monisha has always budgeted, even when it was more challenging to do so. Nannies were also a major expense, but the extra in-home help made the transition back to work after maternity leave manageable—giving her the chance to focus on her career and family equally.

Monisha and her husband share household and family responsibilities on a close to fifty-fifty basis, which is a big reason they feel their partnership works. Her husband does most school drop-offs and pickups since he works remotely. They share cooking and gravitate to individual responsibilities they find easier to do. Monisha, for example, often does the bills, laundry, and daily upkeep of their home. Her husband takes the lead on exterior work and planning kids' activities.

Movie nights, visits to the park, swimming at the pool, and family vacations are many of the experiences Monisha's family share. She and her daughter cheer on her son's soccer team, and her husband is a coach.

At this busy family phase, Monisha most often decompresses with a book or TV show. She would love to get back into working out more regularly, and she is figuring out ways to get into a routine.

Chandra Dhandapani
Former Chief Executive Officer
CBRE | Global Workplace Solutions

Early on in their marriage, Chandra and her husband decided it would be best for their son if one parent had a flexible work arrangement. Chandra was on the corporate career path with a more rigid schedule, including frequent travel, so her husband opted to become a self-employed entrepreneur and then a venture capital investor.

The increased flexibility for Chandra's husband did not eliminate the need for outside childcare. They initially tried daycare, but their son frequently became sick. They ultimately settled on home-based daycare through a live-out nanny. Today her son is in high school and looking forward to college. He also became a good skier as the result of at least one family ski vacation annually.

Though Chandra always stayed on her corporate path, at one point she decided to slow the pace of her career temporarily. When her son turned one, she made a lateral move for about 15 months at the same company to a less demanding operations role with reduced travel and work hours. She continued to learn and grow professionally, and she accepted the more challenging role of Chief Information Officer at a time that was right for her family.

To wind down, Chandra makes dinner for her family most nights. She also works out in the evening during the workweek and meditates every night before falling asleep. She and her husband split household responsibilities—and take on the tasks they naturally prefer. Chandra enjoys cooking, and is happy to have her husband, an engineer, install appliances and technology that make their home fun and secure.

Though her mother is in her eighties and living in India, Chandra still participates in her eldercare decisions. Even thousands of miles away she has all 4 Jobs—including arranging caregiving with her siblings.

Christine DeBiase
Chief Legal Officer, General Counsel
Allstate

With her wife of 24 years, Christine has raised two children—a 23-year-old daughter who is in law school and a 19-year-old son pursuing a career in fashion and music.

When the children were young, the family had one full-time, live-out nanny. In 2013 they moved from New York City to Charlotte, North Carolina, and Christine's wife, Ellen, took a hiatus from her software developer career to stay home with their children. Her wife's at-home presence was especially critical during an 18-month period when Christine was regularly commuting from Charlotte to Austin, Texas, to help care for her mother, who was battling a terminal illness.

Now the family is back in New York City, where they enjoy live music, spending time with friends, and, most important, family Sunday dinners.

To unwind, Christine saves personal time to run, golf, read, and listen to music.

Martine Ferland
Former President and Chief Executive Officer, Mercer
Former Vice Chair, Marsh McLennan

A New York resident, Martine has been married to her husband, Andre, since 1987. Early in their marriage, Andre was an investment banker and then the owner of a digital graphics company. When Martine took on a bigger role leading Towers Perrin's Global Consulting Group, Andre became a full-time painter and sculptor with a very flexible schedule.

Martine also made career changes when her children were young. After her youngest son was born, she left her corporate job as a senior consultant to spend more time with her three children. After one year of not working professionally, she became a freelance consultant—gradually adding hours as her children got older. At the end of this five-year period, she returned to her former employer—at the same level she was when she left.

Now Martine's children are all in their 30s, and as a runner she has the stamina to keep up with three grandchildren. Her daughter, Laurence, is a civil engineer, and another daughter, Corinne, works in digital marketing. Film production is the path that her son, Xavier, chose.

Having grown up in Quebec, Martine and Andre have shared their love of skiing with their family. Travel and hiking have also been family passions, and there were times when their household was very busy: two full-time working parents, three kids, a cat, a dog, and two homes (one a ski cabin).

Caregiving has taken many forms throughout Martine's life, including when her father was diagnosed with terminal cancer. He lived several towns away, and she spent the nine months before his death traveling very frequently to his home. She often reflects on this treasured time, when she would have an early breakfast with her father before heading off to work, putting in a full day at the office, and returning home to a busy family.

Recently retired, Martine is now focused on spending more time with her family and friends and skiing as often as possible.

Anne Foulkes
Senior Vice President and General Counsel
PPG

When Anne, 61, was rising in her career, she had a caregiver who came to their home in Pennsylvania to help with the daily needs of her two daughters.

Now those daughters are 28 and 31. Her oldest graduated from Tufts University with a Chemistry degree and a master's in Biochemical and Molecular Nutrition. She is currently at the University of California pursuing a PhD in Agricultural and Environmental Chemistry—while also working at a start-up focused on food and sustainability. Her youngest received a dual degree in Mathematics and Linguistics from Haverford College, attended graduate school at Harvard, and now teaches Math in Boston.

Anne and her husband of 36 years have always loved traveling, spending time with their daughters at a family lake house, boating, playing tennis, and going to the Jersey shore.

Throughout their marriage, they have split family and household responsibilities almost fifty-fifty (with the help of a house cleaner), but her husband has taken on a bit more since his semi-retirement.

At a very busy point in Anne's career—when she was at the vice president level—her mother developed dementia, making eldercare her fourth job, alongside children, a household, and a career.

In her personal time, Anne exercises five or six days a week—going for a run or a bike ride or working out on the elliptical. To end the days, she reads almost every night before bed.

Janet Foutty
Former US Board Chair
Deloitte
Former Chief Executive Officer
Deloitte Consulting LLP

Janet and her husband of 34 years met in college at Indiana University. Now they live in Chicago, and they have twins—a son and daughter who are 27. Their son is pursuing his PhD at Stanford University, and their daughter is a fourth-grade public school teacher in Portland, Oregon.

Earlier in his career, Janet's husband had a mid-management role at a bank. He then transitioned to academia, becoming a professor of accounting and finance. This allowed him to pursue his passion for teaching and gave him more flexibility to help raise their children and run their household.

In the consulting field, traveling during the week to client sites is part of the job. But when Janet was a mom to newborn twins, she knew it was important to stay local and be close to her children. She set her sights on winning a local client, grew the relationship, and avoided business travel for five years.

Together Janet's family has enjoyed hiking in Colorado and beaches in New Jersey. Ice skating, hiking, and baking are also high on their list of favorite pursuits.

Janet, 57, takes care of her physical and mental well-being every morning before she checks email. Typically, it's a jog, walking her dog Casper, or a Peloton workout.

Aditi Javeri Gokhale
Chief Strategy Officer,
President of Retail Investments and
Head of Institutional Investments
Northwestern Mutual

Technically, Aditi has one child—a 16-year-old son. But she considers her three-year-old Golden/Lab Doodle one of her children as well.

Aditi and her son share a love of tennis—both playing and watching. Her son started lessons at age eight, and when they lived in New York City, they went to the US Open every year. They also traveled to London for the Wimbledon finals in 2022—a trip that played into their love of exploring new countries, trying new cuisines and meeting people from all over the world.

Closer to home in Milwaukee, Aditi enjoys relaxing on the weekends with friends and binging shows on streaming services.

Though career has always been extremely important to Aditi, she stepped back for about a year when her son was an infant to focus on being a mom. At the time she hit pause, she was a Vice President of Marketing at American Express. When she was ready to return to work, she became an entrepreneur, cofounding and acting as Chief Marketing Officer for a digital marketing firm. As is the case with many start-ups, she did not make a huge salary—just enough to support a nanny and some of her living expenses. Through this time, Aditi kept an important hand in the business world, eventually making her way back to corporate life and a C-suite position at Northwestern Mutual.

Jessica Graziano
Chief Financial Officer
U.S. Steel

Connecticut, Florida, and Pennsylvania are places that Jessica, age 51, calls home, and where she spends time with Joe, her husband of 27 years. The couple has two daughters—Olivia, 25, who is pursuing a career in digital marketing, and Mia, 22, who recently graduated from Boston University with a degree in Neuroscience. As young children her daughters were in daycare and spent a lot of time with both sets of grandparents.

Joe began his career in insurance, but then followed passions to become a mental health counselor and professor—both roles that gave him the flexibility to lean into the job of household manager. They've had cleaning and lawn care help for years, which was often a stretch financially, but it protected weekend family time.

Jessica says she and Joe are real partners, but it took them a while to get to a comfortable place. First, they had to make peace with the fact everyone sees the world differently, accepting that what works for them may not work for others. They both come from Italian families where traditional gender roles have not always changed.

As Jessica's career advanced to the C-suite, eldercare for parents and in-laws increased as well. She worked almost exclusively from hospitals when, for 18 months, her father recovered from triple bypass surgery and her mother was treated for a major spinal infection. The interview process for her current role took place from the hospital room or chapel—or in her car.

Most recently, with her company undergoing a massive transformation, Jessica hasn't had a lot of personal time. Any downtime she does have is spent with her immediate and extended families—and they have always enjoyed trips to Disney World and Italy. The best self-care she employs is a solid seven to nine hours of sleep each night.

Christine Hurtsellers
Former Chief Executive Officer, Voya Investment Management
Voya Financial

Alongside building a corporate career, Christine has been the mother to five sons. In the early years, she also shared household responsibilities with her husband, never hiring any help. Now she can more easily afford housecleaning services, and her husband of 38 years, Jim—a retired minister—takes the lead on other chores.

Jim worked on and off throughout Christine's career, so they needed only intermittent daycare and a few years of an au pair. Later, when her business travel escalated, he had more flexibility to stay with their kids. Now those kids range in age from 21 to 34. Her youngest son recently took a gap year from college, one son is a teacher, one son finished his PhD in Religious Studies, and their eldest is a director of photography in the film industry.

Until her recent retirement, Christine never left the workforce, but at one point in her career she took a lower-level job at a new company so she could spend more time with her children. This position was still a good learning experience—she did not lose any significant traction... and eventually reached a C-suite role.

When Christine, age 60, was younger, she ran marathons and triathlons. Now her exercise routine is slightly less ambitious: she gets up at 5:30 a.m. in her Georgia home and takes a Peloton ride or an Orangetheory Fitness class. To ground herself and manage stress, she also meditates every morning.

Jenny Johnson
President and Chief Executive Officer
Franklin Templeton

When Jenny, 60, was rising in her career she had a nanny who helped with the daily needs of her five children—three daughters and two sons. When the kids were still young, she and her husband of 20 years divorced, so she relied on help with housekeeping, cooking, and child-care while she was working.

Now those five kids are between 22 and 32, and all are starting their own career paths.

Jenny and her kids have a special bond and have always loved spending time together. They continue to prioritize family trips, even as the kids have gotten older and she is at one of the busiest points in her career.

Her love of travel is infused into her work life as well. She spends a lot of time on the road meeting with clients and her global team.

In her personal time, Jenny likes to read, draw, and do word puzzles.

Karen Jones
Chief Marketing Officer
Ryder System, Inc.

Karen and her husband of 35 years split their time between Florida and Maine. They've raised a son, Hunter, 33, and built busy professional careers. Karen is also lucky to have 84-year-old parents, who are still active and independent, and she calls her mother her daily touchstone.

When Hunter was in first grade, Karen left her job as a senior manager of marketing to spend more time with him. During this two-year period, she also kept her hand in the marketing world as a consultant. After the hiatus from a demanding corporate job, she managed to return to an even higher position as a director of marketing.

As a working mother, Karen relied on live-in nannies and daycare centers—and summer camps as Hunter got older. In the early years, it was not easy to cover the cost of childcare, and the couple made sacrifices in other areas. Karen's parents and in-laws were also able to pinch hit when their son was sick and could not go to daycare.

Almost 20 years ago, Karen's husband became the family's full-time chef. She calls him "well trained," as he also coordinates all the mechanical and maintenance issues for the household and does a lot of laundry. As the owner of a software company, he has the flexibility to pitch in.

The Jones family loves to sail in the Caribbean or the United States and explore new areas of the world. When Hunter was growing up, Karen and her husband could usually be found at baseball games cheering him on.

With Hunter out of the house now and pursuing a career in sports marketing and sales, Karen and her husband prioritize a dinner with him once a week. On her own, Karen, 60, schedules time to run three mornings a week, and she employs a daily devotional and scripture reading.

Mary K.W. Jones
Former Senior Vice President, General Counsel and
Worldwide Public Affairs
Deere & Company

Other than maternity leaves, Mary, 55, has worked nonstop since college. Because she always had supportive and open-minded bosses and mentors, she was able to have very open and proactive discussions about work structures that would work best for her family. She felt she had the bandwidth to lead a team and travel globally, for example, but she kept an expat assignment off the table.

Mary's ability to keep moving up in her career was due in large part to her supportive husband, Matt, who is the co-owner of an engineering firm. While they were raising young children, both of their jobs required a lot of international travel, which was less than optimal. Matt worked to develop a more local client base, allowing them both to continue their career trajectories without being two parents always on the road. They did all of this with the full range of childcare help—at different times providers who had daycare facilities in their own homes, traditional daycare centers, and individual caregivers who came to their home.

As the couple's children were growing up in their home state of Iowa, their family bonded during travel, sports activities, and volunteering. They have a great group of friends they met through their daughters' volleyball teams, and all the families spend lots of time together.

Mary and Matt, married for 24 years, have never tried to split household responsibilities exactly fifty-fifty, and the distribution of labor has varied over time. The important thing is they do share responsibilities and accept times when one has to do more. They always gave age-appropriate responsibilities to their children, too.

Now these children are older and building their own lives. Their eldest daughter, 25, works in mechanical engineering, and their son in college, 21, is also studying engineering. The couple's youngest daughter, 19, aspires to follow in Mary's footsteps with a career in law.

Though the need to have caregiving for her children is now a distant memory, Mary is in her second phase of caregiving for her parents, who are in their 70s with chronic health issues. Fortunately, her parents live nearby, and she partners with her siblings to give them the support they need.

Jordana Kammerud
Chief Human Resources Officer
Corning Incorporated

When caring for children, it's a blessing when a partner shares household responsibilities. After two years of primary custody when her first child was a toddler (a time she relied on family, friends and caregivers), Jordana found a partner in her husband, Steve, and they've been married for 10 years. Now they have two teenagers—a son and a daughter—and Jordana has a thriving co-parenting partnership with her former husband.

Early in her relationship with Steve, he owned a business, and they traded off staying home when their children were sick. As the middle school and high school years approached, Steve transitioned to independent consulting, increasing his work flexibility and eliminating the need for more daycare.

When Jordana's professional roles intensified, the couple relied more on Steve. He is the first call when issues arise at school, does the pickups and drop-offs, handles the grocery shopping, arranges doctor and repair appointments, shares the cooking responsibilities, and more. Neither partner finds joy in housecleaning, so it's outsourced to make time for other things.

Jordana believes women can achieve fulfillment in both their family and career lives when they're open to exploring a variety of professional roles and choose the roles and tasks that fit where they are in life. Her motto: "You don't always have to say yes—or no—the answer to an offer or request depends on the opportunity and the current family space you're in."

Before she had children, Jordana had an assignment in Germany and jobs requiring greater commitment and travel. After her daughter was born, she turned down an assignment in Australia—daunted by the idea of finding childcare in a foreign country. Before her children were in high school, she took her first Chief Human Resources Officer job requiring extensive travel. Later, when her kids needed her close to home, she took a locally based role. The family moved from Wisconsin to New York when Jordana joined Corning—at a time when her high school children were open to a change.

When Jordana, 47, gets time to herself, she loves to read, spend time with friends and family, and take a walk or hike. Her favorite morning routine is coffee with Steve—even if they only have five minutes. Her family loves to travel, prioritizes dinner together, and enjoys the extremely competitive spirit of family game nights.

Gunjan Kedia
President
U.S. Bancorp

In the workforce without any pause, Gunjan, 53, has experienced all 4 Jobs—often at the same time. She raised two sons, and care for her parents and in-laws has involved a terminal illness, general life administration, and emotional support.

When her mother was battling breast cancer, Gunjan had just switched jobs and moved to Boston, fortuitously near her mother's treatments. As she was settling into a new home and job at the Executive Vice President level, she had the added responsibility of seeing her mother through her final years.

As immigrants, Gunjan and her husband haven't had a lot of family nearby, so they've invested substantially in household help. In the early years, the family had a live-out nanny (and sometimes two to cover extended hours) and babysitters. They also invested in house cleaning and yard work services. This all came at a big price, but to offset those expenses they bought a smaller and more manageable home.

Gunjan's husband has always had an equally demanding work life—he founded a business that was eventually sold to a large company. Now he's a professor at Carnegie Mellon University, and Gunjan sees her husband of 28 years as part of the trend of partners doing more at home.

Traveling is one of the big ways that Gunjan's family spends special time together, and that includes an annual trip to India. At home (she divides her time between Pennsylvania and Minnesota), she rises early and reads news and documents for the day ahead. Most days she leaves the office by 6:00 p.m. (unless she has a client dinner, or she is on the road). She stops reading emails at least one hour before bed, and instead stretches with yoga, reads for pleasure, listens to music or watches a show. On the weekends she clears her head by lifting weights and running.

Shannon Lapierre
Former Chief Communications Officer
Stanley Black & Decker

When Shannon's career became more demanding, she approached her husband, Brian, and young daughter, Danielle, about hiring a nanny and other household help. After interviewing several candidates, her family nixed the idea because they didn't want an outsider in their home every day.

Instead, they came up with these solutions: Brian found a more flexible sales role so he could be available during the week; they hired local high school students part-time; and they found a housecleaner to fill in the gaps. Over the years, Brian worked part-time, full-time, and not at all to accommodate the demands of Shannon's job and their daughter's activities.

Brian held the role of "primary caregiver"—picking Danielle up from school when she was sick, driving her to after-school activities and appointments, and making meals (it helps that he is a trained chef). Shannon could then travel as needed for work, stay late for emergencies, and commute more than an hour each way to her office. She was able to advance in her career by being physically available in the office, a necessity in those career building/pre-pandemic/pre-remote-work years.

After an incredibly busy work period, Shannon, now 52, would pull Danielle from childcare or school to "play hooky" as a way of navigating working-mother guilt. But Danielle was no stranger to Shannon's work life—she would often spend time in Shannon's office on Friday afternoons or during school vacation weeks. As she got older, Danielle was often Shannon's "date" at charitable events, galas, and other corporate events.

And with all that exposure to the corporate world, Danielle graduated from Belmont University in Nashville with a bachelor's in Music Business. She has followed her mom's advice: "You'll work for a long time, so try hard to find the perfect Venn diagram intersection—something you are passionate about (music), something you are good at (business), and something someone will pay you to do (music business)."

Now, the family has followed Danielle to Nashville, enjoying living in a new and vibrant city while Shannon is on her second career sabbatical.

Martha Leiper
Chief Investment Officer
Unum Group

Martha married young, knowing she found someone she not only loved, but also would be an involved partner and father. Early in their 40-year marriage, they decided only Martha would climb the corporate ladder, while her husband would pursue a rewarding career in development at a parochial school.

This doesn't mean Martha has taken a pass at their home in Tennessee. She and her husband have always had a fifty-fifty partnership, covering chores, financial management, and family decisions. One example is mealtime: Martha loves to cook, and her husband cleans up—what she calls "a match made in heaven."

Beyond the kitchen, Martha loves a clean house but hates spending precious weekends cleaning. She splurged on the cost of a housekeeper when her children were young and found it well worth the expense (even though money was initially tight).

As the primary breadwinner, Martha never had the luxury of taking a hiatus. She did slow down temporarily after her second child was born, turning down a great opportunity requiring too much travel. It was a tough but wise decision for her young family—and her own mental health.

When her children were young, Martha found a woman who had in-home daycare. She cared for all of Martha's children like they were her own—from 10-weeks-old until preschool and then part-time until kindergarten.

Now Martha is 61 and her children are adults building their own careers. Their oldest son, 36, is married and in the US Army Judge Advocate General's Corps (JAG Corps). A daughter, 31, who is married with a three-year-old son, is a senior business analyst for a national distributing company. Martha's youngest son, 26, is in customer service for a large retailer and not yet married.

As Martha passed the stage of caring for young children, she took on responsibilities for aging parents. Fortunately, her parents planned well for retirement and could afford an assisted living facility. While Martha had a demanding job as senior vice president of a large financial services company, she managed their finances and transition from assisted living to memory care. Whenever Martha was in a particularly busy period, her husband stepped in and helped with her parents, too.

To foster close relationships in their next generation, Martha and her husband take frequent beach vacations with lots of cousins and extended family. On a more regular basis, her downtime includes early morning exercise at the gym.

Patricia L. Lewis
Executive Vice President and Chief Sustainability Officer
UnitedHealth Group

For 10 years Patricia was a single parent, raising a son while she was rising in her career. She had limited opportunity to travel for business during this time, which initially limited her career mobility. At first, she enrolled her son in daycare, and then when she reached the Vice President level, she felt she could afford a live-in nanny.

Then Patricia got married and her wife brought three more young children into her life. They've created a blended family that includes three sons, one daughter, and three grandsons. Now Patricia's son is 23, and her three stepchildren are 33, 30, and 25.

After a career in healthcare, Patricia's wife, Sherron, stopped working to manage their home and busy schedules. Now empty nesters, they share household responsibilities.

An avid reader, Patricia also exercises three to five times a week for her health and to reduce stress. She loves spending time with friends and family on the weekends.

For five years Patricia had a second caregiving job—tending to her mother before she passed away. She cherished the time with her mother, while she was also caring for her career at the C-suite level.

Mary Mack
Former Chief Executive Officer, Consumer & Small Business Banking
Wells Fargo

Mary, 62, and her husband have been married for 39 years and together for 41. The South Carolina residents have always had a fifty-fifty arrangement with household responsibilities. She washes clothes; he folds. He preps food; she cooks. She unloads the dishwasher; he puts the clean dishes away. And they both take care of their four dogs.

The couple has three daughters. Their 28-year-old is a pediatric nurse at a low-income family clinic, and their 32-year-old is a Title 1 fourth-grade teacher. Their first daughter, Mary Warner, passed away in 2014 at the age of 23. When the girls were young, they were cared for by a nanny, who was like family and helped run the household for 25 years—making it possible for Mary to work and be an avid fan at her daughters' gymnastics and volleyball events.

Always very involved in her children's lives, Mary paced her career according to her family's needs. She and her husband (who runs a law firm next door to their home) decided they would not move for her job when their daughters were young. This meant turning down bigger job offers in other locations. She also negotiated a four-day workweek when her second child was born 25 months after her first. This arrangement lasted for several years and did not impede her career advancement. She returned to full-time work and was promoted within a year.

For several years, while Mary was running various businesses, she and her three siblings shared responsibility for their aging mother. During this time, she also had another big caregiving job with children still at home.

A very early riser, Mary always started her work day at 4:45 a.m. to run and exercise (including Barre and F45 Training) before the commute to her office. She also loves to read and has a couple of books going at all times.

Now early into her retirement, she is focused on helping Wells Fargo build an alumni network, serving the community (including projects honoring the memory of her daughter, Mary Warner), and being a new grandmother.

Kris Malkoski
Segment CEO, Learning & Development
Newell Brands

Like mother, like daughter—and son. Consumer packaged-goods expertise runs deep in the Malkoski family. Kris's work involves iconic brands like Sharpie, Paper Mate, Elmer's, and Graco. Her daughter, 33, and one of her twin sons, 31, are also pursuing careers focused on consumer brands. Her husband of 38 years was the CEO of two consumer food-related companies (and is now a private equity consultant). Their other twin son works in computer gaming.

With three adult children on their own now, Kris and her husband share their Georgia household responsibilities evenly. When their kids were young, Kris managed about 90 percent while balancing a career as a senior executive. They had no family nearby, and Kris knew if she wanted to pursue her career aspirations and give her best self to her family, she needed help—so she hired a nanny and a housekeeper. When she was home in the evenings and on weekends, she could dedicate her time 100 percent to her husband and kids.

As a family, they took many vacations, visited grandparents for a week at a time, did a lot of weekend arts and crafts projects, and supported each other's team sports.

When Kris was President and Chief Operating Officer at Pharmaceutical Corporation of America (PCA), she left her position to be home full-time with her twin boys. She returned to work after a two-year hiatus, and took a more junior role at a smaller company. She did not let this discourage her, and within three years, she returned to a position that was comparable to her pre-hiatus job.

Kris is up by 5:00 a.m. and starts in on her regimen of 10,000 steps a day. (She used to run before she had a knee replacement.) Always reading, she also listens to audio books (and finishes about two books a week). Cooking is a way for her to unwind, and she's always planning trips to visit her kids and grandchild.

Liz Mazzotta
Chief Administrative Officer
Mutual of Omaha

When your partner owns a business, there's a bit more schedule flexibility for a two-career couple. That's been the case for Liz and her husband of 28 years. While Liz has risen in her corporate career, her husband has had a real estate business developing housing in various states.

Liz, 66, and her husband share household responsibilities—Liz takes the lead on grocery shopping and meals, for example, and one of her husband's main responsibilities is care of their cat. Starting early in their careers, the couple has had a housekeeper once a week.

When their two children were young, the family enjoyed beach vacations and spent a lot of time at soccer games and swim meets in their home state of Nebraska. On her own, Liz is an avid reader and exercises early in the morning—two days a week with a virtual trainer and walking with friends as many days as possible. Liz also finds it extremely gratifying to volunteer at a homeless shelter serving Sunday meals, and she serves on the shelter's board of directors.

In the early years, Liz's son had after-school care at his elementary school, and her daughter went to Montessori from age 18 months to three years. Now her son, 35, works in his father's real estate business, and their daughter, 26, is a law student.

As Liz's career became more demanding, responsibilities also increased for her aging parents. Both had cancer (her father's diagnosis came when her daughter was a baby), and her mother was also dealing with the disease when her children were young. Liz traveled frequently from Omaha to South Dakota, where her parents lived—when she was also caring for her own family, household, and career. She rotated caregiving with her two sisters (one retired and one a doctor), which was helpful in balancing family demands.

Denise Merle
Chief Administrative Officer
Weyerhaeuser

At every age (and now at age 60), Denise's mantra has been "make things easy." Don't drive far to get things done. (She stopped driving to another city to get her hair cut.) Cut down on last-minute confusion. (Organize all family activities for the week so you're ready to go each morning.) Don't spend a lot of time figuring out what to have to dinner. (Meal plan on the weekends.) And most of all, hire a housekeeper as soon as you can afford it!

Compromise is also a key word in Denise's life. She and her husband of 31 years have shared household responsibilities pretty equally, but since he has had a demanding career as well, they flex and help each other out. Now retired, her husband first had a career in in finance, and he later worked as an adjunct professor.

The couple has two children—a daughter, 28, who studied Chemistry and is a production engineer for a helicopter company, and a son, 26, who graduated from Columbia University Law School. When they were young, Denise used many different childcare resources, including daycare, nannies, and afterschool care. She could work flexible hours, too, which allowed her to pick her children up from school.

Eldercare was also a job for Denise—she spent a lot of time caring for her parents during the last stages of their lives. When her mother was going through cancer treatment, Denise was a Chief Internal Auditor. She had great colleagues and worked for a company that gave her the time and flexibility to be with her mother.

Living in the state of Washington, Denise's family has taken advantage of outdoor activities. She and her husband taught their kids to ski at a young age, which led to annual family ski trips. They also spent lots of time on the water, boating in the Pacific Northwest. Traveling to different parts of the world was on the family agenda, too.

Exercise is important "me time" for Denise. Now that she's an empty nester, she moved from a morning to an evening exercise schedule that is a great transition from work to home. She also loves to read, cook, and tend to her vegetable garden.

Marie Myers
Executive Vice President and Chief Financial Officer
Hewlett Packard Enterprise

A native of Australia and resident of Texas, Marie, 56, is married to an entrepreneur and CEO of a small company. With two busy careers, Marie says it takes both of them to keep their household running smoothly.

The couple is in the busy child-rearing years—with 12-year-old fraternal twins and a 16-year-old daughter. When the children were younger, Marie invested more than a third of her paycheck to pay for live-in nannies, who acted as the family's house manager.

After her twins were born, Marie took a brief sabbatical to focus on her family. By the time the twins were walking, she was back in the workforce full time and her career picked up momentum.

As a family, time outside work and school revolves around the many sports activities the children pursue. They love to travel, and they all give back by volunteering in the community.

To have time to herself, Marie gets up early every morning to exercise (she enjoys spinning), prepare for the day, read, and steal a few moments to make jewelry.

Kimberly Paige
Chief Marketing Officer
BET Networks

Kimberly is based in Atlanta and works in New York City. She has a son in college (majoring in Business) and a daughter who lives and works in New York City.

Early in her career, she negotiated a four-day workweek so she could spend more time with her children. At the time, her daughter had just started middle school. Though Kimberly worked fewer days, her responsibilities did not decrease. The extra day at home simply allowed her to be more active at her children's schools and have a longer weekend with her family.

When her children were young, the family had a full-time nanny who later worked part-time as they became more independent. While working in the C-suite, Kimberly partnered with her sister to take care of their mother at the end of her life.

Now divorced, Kimberly follows this mantra: live life with meaning. She is very intentional about creating moments that matter with family and friends. This can include something as simple as a walk, a family vacation, or a family dinner when they talk about everything from big life issues to the silliest of things.

Penny Pennington
Managing Partner
Edward Jones

At age 60, "active" is Penny's moniker. At the helm of a Fortune 500 firm, she prioritizes her health and well-being, something she hopes is an example to her nearly 54,000 colleagues. On weekdays, Penny is up by 5:15 a.m. to meditate and exercise. Even on weekends, she spends her mornings running or strength training. And, although she's health-driven, she's not a fan of deprivation: every night she has a glass of cabernet and the darkest chocolate she can find.

Penny is also passionate about fully leaning into her purpose. From her early career as a financial adviser to now, helping people build and invest in their long-term financial futures has always been at the forefront of her days.

She lives with her husband, Mike, in Missouri. He retired as a corporate banker after 27 years and then became "the rock who makes all things possible." The couple has two daughters—young women Penny learns from every day. She loves to spend time with her family, especially outdoors—hiking, running, and visiting parks and museums. Some of her memorable moments include completing a 590-mile bike event, camping at the bottom of the Grand Canyon, and riding down Hawaii's rugged Haleakalā National Park trails.

Jill Penrose
Chief People and Company Services Officer
The J.M. Smucker Co.

With two sons in their mid and late teens and three aging parents and in-laws, Jill knows what it means to have 4 Jobs. Her personal experiences have shaped how she approaches her professional work—encouraging all leaders to show empathy, thoughtfulness, and understanding for the many life roles all employees play.

One personal experience especially meaningful to Jill was the time she cared for her mother, who was battling breast cancer. This was when Jill was in a senior-level role at Smucker, and she had opportunities for continued advancement. Jill worried about taking time away to be with her mother, but her leadership encouraged her to do so. After her mother passed, she returned to her role and was promoted to the officer level shortly thereafter.

In addition to her professional leadership and making time to care for parents, Jill's primary caregiving role has been raising two sons along with her husband, Mike, an entrepreneur with a similarly demanding career. After the birth of their eldest son, Jill was able to coordinate a more flexible schedule for a short period to allow her to balance all aspects of her life.

Once the couple was ready to invest in childcare, they were pleased to find a nanny who was able to cover early mornings and evenings when necessary.

Today, with her sons getting older, Jill is transparent about her own life experiences as she supports the needs of employees across the organization who are caring for aging parents and growing children. She believes organizations that support employees who have 4 Jobs will ultimately see the greatest success.

Jennifer Piepszak
Co-Chief Executive Officer, Commercial and Investment Bank
JPMorganChase

Jennifer and her husband met in high school and married after college. They've had a strong partnership for more than 25 years, and the New Jersey residents have three sons ranging in age from 16 to 20 (two in college and one in high school).

When the boys were young, they had a live-in nanny, and the family enjoyed lots of travel, skiing, and days at the beach.

Jenn, age 54, prioritizes exercise and spending time with family and friends.

Smita Pillai
Chief Diversity, Equity and Inclusion Officer
Regeneron Pharmaceuticals

Now in the proud 40s club, Smita looks back to when she was newly married and had a very successful global marketing career in Dubai. Her husband asked her to move to Jacksonville, Florida, so he could pursue technology opportunities in the ripe U.S. market. It wasn't an easy decision, and it led to a short break in her career (and a slight step backward) as she got her bearings and found a new job. In hindsight, the move and career break were advantageous: she reached the C-suite within 15 years, and her 22-year marriage is still going strong.

Now Smita's husband is an artificial intelligence leader with a demanding research role. He does have schedule flexibility to drive their children (a 13-year-old son and 9-year-old twin daughters) to afternoon activities. This gives Smita time to get home and prepare dinner.

When their children were younger, they had live-out nannies and a lot of help from visiting grandparents. They are slowly transitioning to a more self-sufficient household—other than lawn and snow removal services. Smita and her husband share most household responsibilities, and their children contribute in age-appropriate ways, too. Their son, for example, is a budding chef, enthusiastically cooking dinner at least twice a week for the family (after his homework is done).

Living in New York State, the whole family enjoys cooking together and staying fit through frequent hikes. Smita and her husband also work out in the morning (at Orangetheory Fitness) before the chaos of school and work sets in. The family travels to a new country every couple of years, and even with their young children they have in-depth discussions about exhibits they visit at the world's most compelling museums.

Suzanne Powers
Founder CEO, Powers Creativity
Former Global Chief Product Officer, McCann Worldgroup
Former Chair, FutureBrand

Suzanne is a 50-ish woman who thrives on the energy and ideas that come from bringing people together to solve problems, celebrate life, and create a more optimistic world. Her work and home life have always been a conscious blend—sometimes harmonious and sometimes fractured. But she believes we grow and flourish from life's ups (exploring the world, spending time with her kids, meeting her life partner) and downs (divorce, single mom challenges, work conundrums). It's all life, she says, and it's what makes us amazing, interesting, and ever-evolving beings.

In her personal life, Suzanne is a mother, wife, daughter, sister, and friend. She and her first husband divorced amicably when their twin boys were eight years old, and they maintain a healthy co-parenting relationship. She shares a full life with her second husband, Steve (married for six years and together for 10) and their blended family. Suzanne's twins are now 22 (heading to the advertising and marketing business), and her husband's children are in their late 20s and living outside of London. The blended family of six loves to travel together, and they still do at least one trip a year as a full family. Bringing the two families together has been one of Suzanne's most rewarding experiences.

The couple lives in New York City, and they have a country cottage in Connecticut, where they go to slow down, recharge, and unplug from the always-on city culture. Their dog, Fitzgerald, is a funny and eccentric Golden Doodle that truly thinks he's human, too.

Suzanne's immediate family lives on both coasts, and they are all sun-seekers, which she attributes to growing up in Montreal. She loves to read and keep her body moving for mental well-being and physical vitality.

Someone recently asked, "Do you ever stop worrying about your kids?" Suzanne and her husband answered, "Absolutely NOT," but they agree that above the constant hum of parental concern, there's the much louder music of love, laughter, and never-ending learning.

Gregg Renfrew
Entrepreneur
Founder and Chief Executive Officer
Beautycounter

When Gregg graduated from college, her mother handed her a briefcase monogrammed with her initials and a check for $5,000. Her mother said she was proud of her, and that Gregg was now capable of being on her own. Gregg had been raised knowing the importance of a woman standing on her own two feet financially. Her father got sick when she was 14 and died of cancer when she was in her 20s, leaving her mother as the sole provider, which she did successfully, but not without struggles.

As a young couple working full time and raising children in New York City, it was always a balancing act for Gregg and her husband, Mark Hancock. When she was a new mother, Gregg quickly embraced the mindset you *can* have it all, just not necessarily all in one day. She repeats this motto to parents who struggle to find a way to take care of everything, or to do it all well. Prioritization, and knowing some days are more focused on family and other days more focused on work, will help you thrive as a mother, partner, and woman.

Gregg and Mark continue to focus on being present for their kids, now 19, 17, and 15. Communication has always been key, especially now when children are older and the very special times they are all together as a family are fewer and farther between. Gregg believes you don't have to be there every single moment to be a good parent, but you need to be there for the most important moments. This helps children gain confidence and independence.

Stephanie Richard
Chief Audit Executive
Ally Financial

When 51-year-old Stephanie winds down, she likes to exercise, read, bake, and volunteer. Four days during the workweek, she gets up at 5:15 a.m., drinks a cup of coffee in silence, and thinks about how the day will unfold. Then she rides the Peloton for 30 minutes. On the fifth day, she skips the exercise and gives herself the gift of drinking *two cups* of coffee in silence.

Living in North Carolina, Stephanie has always enjoyed bike riding and weekend hikes with her children. Her son, 19, is at Clemson University pursuing a degree in Financial Management. Her daughter, 16, is in high school with current aspirations to become a sports broadcaster and sideline reporter.

Married for 21 years, Stephanie calls her husband the house manager, chauffeur, and chef. He was formerly a marketing director for a major automotive manufacturer, and in the early years, when they were both in the workforce, they relied on daycare for their young children. Her husband left his job to take the lead at home when their children were five and two years old. The couple has always shared household responsibilities about fifty-fifty.

One thing is for sure—they have a cleaning service every two weeks. Through the years, Stephanie says she refused to spend precious weekends cleaning the house—no matter what she might have had to cut down on, like eating out or buying new clothes.

Like so many other women, Stephanie indeed has 4 Jobs. In addition to her professional work, raising children, and running the household with her husband, she is also a health advocate for her parents, who are in their mid-70s and early 80s.

Marie Robinson
Former Chief Supply Chain Officer
Sysco

In addition to being a committed partner of 22 years to her husband, Bob, Marie has truly had four roles throughout her adult life: working hard at a career in supply chain management; serving as mom to two boys and three stepchildren; contributing to the management of her household; and being the key care coordinator for her late father and now her mother.

When Marie was a young single mother at a key time in her career, her parents took an early retirement and spent five years supporting her family, moving with them three times. Then she met her husband, her parents "retired," and after a couple shaky starts she and Bob found a wonderful live-out nanny, who evolved into their household manager when the boys were older.

In 2013, just as their youngest was leaving the nest, Marie was diagnosed with breast cancer. Bob left his job to be her caretaker for the year, then retired early. Marie fully recovered and runs to stay healthy. Bob shifted to primary household leader, supporting Marie's career moves—alongside wonderful housekeepers, gardeners, and the like.

Marie retired from her full-time executive role at Sysco and is now an independent board director for three companies. She and Bob enjoy traveling the country with their two dogs in an RV—seeing friends, family, and sunsets along the way.

Julie Rosen
President
Bath & Body Works

Married 30-plus years, Julie calls her husband, Jeffrey, an amazing partner and the biggest sponsor of her career. They do everything as a team, sharing many family responsibilities. However, her husband does more of the work at home: all the cooking, errands, and organization of travel and outings.

When Julie's sons were young, the family had a full-time nanny who stayed with them for 12 years. The trio of Julie, Jeffrey, and the nanny provided a solid foundation for her sons, now in their 20s and pursuing real estate private credit and entertainment careers.

Early on in their marriage, the couple decided one of them needed work flexibility. Julie was in the corporate world and traveled for work, and Jeffrey was an attorney at a law firm. Jeffrey went the entrepreneurial route, becoming a small business owner in the employee benefits field.

Julie did pivot her career when her sons were in first and second grade. To spend more time with them, she started her own consulting firm. This entrepreneurial venture spanned four years and then she returned to her former employer—at the same level she was at when she left.

During the time that Julie has led Bath & Body Works, she took on the fourth job—caring for her mother, who had pancreatic cancer. From her home in Columbus, Ohio she traveled to her mother's home in Florida (where she was able to work remotely and help her sister care for their mother) and spent one week there each month for nine months.

Julie is a firm believer in separating professional and personal pursuits so she can be present and focused on each important aspect of her life. While that can be hard at times, keeping separate phones has been a big help. To run all aspects of her life smoothly, she gets up by 5:30 a.m. and exercises for at least an hour. At age 59, she loves yoga, Pilates, and spinning—and she meditates most days. On weekends she enjoys hiking, going to concerts, and visiting museums. Travel has also been a priority in her family, and they have focused on seeing the world together.

Dana Rosenfeld
Firm Managing Partner
Kelley Drye & Warren LLP

Dana believes in leaving the office behind at the end of the day. Of course, issues arise during the off hours that sometimes need attention, but she generally tries not to rehash the day's events in her head. Her mantra is to keep moving forward.

Married since 1988, Dana and her husband, Eric Biel, have two adult sons—a 33-year-old university librarian and a 30-year-old real estate professional. When the boys were young, the couple first took them to daycare and then later employed a nanny. Once the kids were older, Dana took advantage of after-school programs.

Both Dana and Eric have had demanding careers—Eric, a lawyer, has had various senior policy roles in government and nonprofit organizations sometimes requiring extensive international travel. When Dana's sons were young, she worked a reduced-hours schedule as a lawyer at the Federal Trade Commission and negotiated a 75 percent work arrangement when she later joined a large law firm. She did not return to full-time work until she joined Kelley Drye & Warren as a partner in 2009.

Along with raising children, running a household, and being one of the only women to manage a national law firm, Dana spends time with her aging mother, who lives nearby. Her mother-in-law passed away after a long period of decline, requiring frequent travel to Cleveland from Dana's Maryland home.

Dana's family has enjoyed lots of travel and ski trips with other families. They've also attended many sporting events, including her sons' games.

On her own, Dana prioritizes quality time with people she cares about. She exercises on an elliptical every morning, reads, enjoys theater (especially Broadway musicals)—and good meals with good conversation.

Note: Since this biography was written, Dana's husband lost a long and hard-fought battle with cancer. As she adjusts to very changed circumstances in her personal life, she continues to be actively engaged in her work as Managing Partner of the firm.

Linda Rutherford
Chief Administration Officer
Southwest Airlines

Texas residents Linda and her husband, Mike, recently celebrated their thirtieth wedding anniversary. They credit marriage longevity to a true partnership and a purposeful sharing of life, family and household responsibilities. This has made two high-level careers possible—while Linda was rising in the corporate ranks, Mike, now retired, worked for 30-plus years as a subject matter expert for an international business.

Linda, age 57, is the resident planner and scheduler, handles day-to-day tidying, and makes sure everyone gets a birthday gift on time. Mike is the chef, managing most dinner plans (cooking or takeout). When their children were growing up, he shuttled their children to activities at all hours, earning "Superstar Dad" status, according to Linda. They agreed long ago to outsource the most time-consuming activities that interfered with family time—like house cleanings every two weeks.

When their children were young, they first went to an in-home daycare, and then a daycare facility and Montessori before kindergarten in public school. Now Matthew, 26, works for a sports marketing firm after graduating from Rice University. Allison, 24, is pursuing a career in public health, after earning a master's degree in public health at Tulane University and a BS from the University of Texas, Austin.

With a self-described "manic work ethic," Linda has worked basically nonstop since college. She believes "it takes a village," and was fortunate to have nearby grandparents, aunts, and uncles always eager available to help before, during and after her two maternity leaves. She also aims for work–life harmony—rather than perfect balance—giving herself grace when there is a period of a less than equal work–life blend.

Being the primary caregiver for aging parents has made achieving harmony more challenging. When her mother became ill, Linda had just been promoted to Executive Vice President, and she was her mother's medical and financial custodian, organizing all doctors and medical care before her death in 2020.

Benefiting from her airline employer, Linda's family has traveled the world experiencing new cultures and cuisines. They share weeklong family vacations to a new place each year—enjoying Hawaiian beaches, Canadian mountains, and many international locations.

A huge sports fan and proud Texas Tech University alum, Linda loves to watch football and basketball. She and Mike also enjoy community gardening—experimenting with vegetable varietals and donating all produce to local food pantries.

Sharon Ryan
Former Senior Vice President and General Counsel
International Paper

After 36 years in corporate America, Sharon, 65, retired in 2021 to spend more time with her husband of 30-plus years at their home in Tennessee.

The couple has two daughters, ages 28 and 27. The eldest is an aesthetician, and the youngest is a mechanical engineer who moved into human resources.

Everyone gathers regularly on Sunday evenings—a family dinner priority that started years ago. Even though Sharon was very busy working, she still cooked dinner most evenings. She and her husband also volunteered regularly for school and sports events.

Midway through Sharon's career, her husband retired early from a computer sales position after relocating several times with Sharon's job at International Paper. Bill said, "I have a job and you have a career, so I'll do what's needed to support you." Along with her husband's contributions, they had help with cleaning and some childcare—but he was the household manager while Sharon was working. (Sharon says that the minute she retired he suddenly found lots of hobbies.)

When the girls were young, the family had a live-in nanny with whom they are still close. Sharon has traveled with this former nanny to Poland, and the nanny brings her husband and children to visit the Ryans' lake house every summer.

In addition to raising children, Sharon shared an eldercare job with her two sisters. Her parents, who lived in California, passed away in their 90s, and for several years (while she was in her General Counsel role), she helped from afar. She ordered their groceries, paid bills, helped organize eldercare, and eventually moved her father to a care facility. At the same time, she was taking care of her best friend, who was terminally ill.

Sharon always worked full time but made sure to carve out time for herself. She's not an early riser by nature but adapted when a boss got to the office at 5:00 a.m. Her workday routine was to get seven to eight hours of sleep, rise at 7:00 a.m., care for her dogs, and have coffee with her husband by the pool. She's an avid gardener and loves to sew and read historical novels.

Travel has also been a high priority: she has taken regular trips with a "girls' group" (recently to New Zealand). Now retired, she and her husband are working toward their goal of visiting all major US national parks.

Raj Seshadri
Chief Commercial Payments Officer
Mastercard

Raj is very close to her two sons, who are now in their 20s—one in college and one in the workforce. When her sons were young, both she and her husband had demanding careers with a fifty-fifty partnership when it came to household and family responsibilities.

As a family they were fortunate to have longevity in their caregiver—a loving nanny for 16 years, who became as close as a grandmother to the boys. They also had au pairs for eight years and a housekeeper who came once a week. They prioritized time to make sure at least Raj or her husband was home with the boys every evening, and they were committed to attending major activities in the boys' lives—music performances, athletic games, and other school events. Weekends were devoted to spending time together—playing board and card games, physical activities like biking and skiing, growing fruits and vegetables, and cooking fun dinners.

At one point in her career, Raj reduced her work hours to make more time for her family. Later in her career, her father, now in his 90s, had major surgery, and she was his primary caregiver—a life phase when Raj got a glimpse of the future challenge of juggling 4 Jobs.

Through the years Raj's family enjoyed traveling to new destinations for adventurous vacations, following various athletics teams, and enjoying musical performances and theater. For her own pleasure, Raj, in her 50s, loves to exercise, read, cook, knit, and spend time with friends and family.

Amy Shore
Executive Vice President and Chief Customer Officer
Nationwide

After the whirlwind of raising two children, Amy and her husband, Alan, who have been married 37 years, are empty nesters enjoying their time together. From their home in Ohio, they walk their dog every evening and enjoy many dinners and cultural events with friends. With her adult children now settled, Amy has no problem reading herself to sleep at night.

When their children were young, Amy was on her corporate career trajectory, and Alan was a research biochemist. The couple enrolled their children in daycare and at other times had a daytime nanny. Then, when the children were ages two and seven, Alan decided to become a stay-at-home dad.

As a family, they've always enjoyed lots of outdoor activities, big family vacations, and traveling frequently to visit relatives. Though they traveled avidly for pleasure, Amy put boundaries around her job mobility. For the nine concurrent years her children were in high school, Amy was not open to relocation. This gave her children the opportunity to stay in the same school for all their high school years.

Now well out of high school, their children (Caroline, 34, and Jordan, 29) are building their careers. Caroline owns a horse farm, and Jordan is an industrial hygiene consultant.

Because Amy, now in her 50s, has continued to work full time, Alan takes the lead on household responsibilities, with a division of about seventy-thirty. He does all the shopping, cooking, and yard work. Amy does most of the laundry, cooks occasionally, and cleans in between the housekeeper's biweekly visits. The decision to have help with the cleaning was made when they were both working and discussions about who should do what were a source of friction. Overall, the couple believes everyone should pitch in, so when their kids were in the house, they had chores, too.

Through the years Amy has experienced all 4 Jobs—including eldercare for her father, who battled cancer during the last year of his life. This was when she had big responsibilities at the Vice President level, and her teenage children also needed her attention. Thankfully, the family had a strong village of support.

Mindy Simon
Global Chief Operating Officer
Aon

Nebraska resident Mindy Simon has been married to her husband, Jon, for 26 years, and they have four children, who now range in age from 9 to 16. They enjoy living in a quiet lake community close to the the farms they grew up on. They still visit one of the family farms for adventures and to share life lessons with the kids.

Before their children were in school, they relied primarily on daycare resources. The couple also hired a housecleaner through the years to help manage their household, and they share tasks of groceries and cooking. Jon now stays home and has the primary role of transporting the kids to school and their many activities, and he does all the laundry (which adds up quickly with four kids).

When Mindy was at the Senior Vice President and Chief Information Officer levels, she also had an eldercare job when her father was ill with Parkinson's. This is why she says there are times at work when she needs to be a mother, wife, sister, and daughter and there are times at home she needs to be an executive. From her farm roots, she's always known the convergence of work and life.

Mindy tries to balance time over the course of a year, not within a single day. She makes sure to take time off for exploration and discovery as a family. They recently spent a year in London, which enabled travel to many countries. Back in the United States they enjoy skiing, national parks, camping, and road trips as well as spending time with family and friends at their lake house.

Mindy continues to work on ways to unwind and have greater mindfulness. She exercises regularly, loves to cook and bake, and frequents local bookstores while traveling to add great books to her reading list.

Jacinth Smiley
Executive Vice President and Chief Financial Officer
Hormel Foods

When Jacinth's son was a baby, her husband—an entrepreneur who eventually sold his business to have the flexibility to support her frequent career moves—would travel with her (son in tow) so he could feed their son with the breastmilk she pumped.

Her husband's contributions to all aspects of family life in Minnesota has continued at a high level: he does all of the grocery shopping and cooking, takes care of his own laundry, and handles some house cleaning. Jacinth also cleans and does her laundry on the weekends. It's a seventy-five-twenty-five split (with her husband taking on the bulk of the household responsibilities), which gives Jacinth the freedom she needs to pursue her demanding career.

Jacinth has always taken her motherhood role as seriously—especially negotiating a phased-in return to work after her maternity leave. She started with half days the first month. Then for another 18 months, she kept to eight-hour days in the office, leaving at a reasonable hour to spend time with her baby. When necessary, she got back online to work in the evenings.

Although her husband worked from home, they relied on daycare during their son's early years until her husband became the full-time caretaker. Since the family moved every 18 to 24 months for Jacinth's job, their son got used to many different environments. This is the reason she believes her son, now 18, is so adaptable to new situations in daily life and when they travel the world.

During off hours, Jacinth, age 55, prioritizes exercise. She rises at 4:00 a.m. and starts with a 90-minute exercise session: a 6- to 10-mile run plus weight training. On the weekends she gets up a little later—at 6:00 a.m.— and goes on 10-mile runs, along with HIIT, weight training, and yoga.

Jill Timm
Chief Financial Officer
Kohl's

Jill and her husband both pursued busy careers in finance, making it incredibly helpful that she could drop her two daughters off at the Kohl's on-site childcare. Her husband picked them up at night, and when one of their daughters was sick, they decided who would stay home. If her husband was in the middle of quarter end, she would stay home, and if Jill had an important meeting, her husband would stay home. This give-and-take has been a hallmark of their 27-year marriage.

When their daughters were older, she quickly learned it took a village to run their family. Her neighbors got her daughters on the school bus three days a week, and Jill started her workday later the other two days. Her in-laws got the girls off the bus and to after-school activities.

Now these daughters are in college: the eldest is a senior at University of Wisconsin–Madison, and the youngest is at DePaul University, playing basketball alongside her studies. As a family, they've always enjoyed traveling, including beach vacations and summer trips abroad and across the United States.

Jill's husband retired from his finance career in 2019 and now enjoys volunteering for Habitat for Humanity and running a handyman business. This change gave him more schedule flexibility to help with the girls, their aging parents, and the household.

While Jill was in her current role, her father was diagnosed with Bulbar ALS, and she and her brother shared responsibility for all his healthcare needs. Since her father passed away in 2022, she has helped her 81-year-old mother with financial and healthcare needs, as well as a move to a senior living facility.

To decompress from busy days, Jill, 51, exercises four to five days a week after work, including running and interval workouts. The Wisconsin resident also likes to read, attend her daughter's sporting events, and spend lots of time with friends and family.

Anne White
President, Lilly Neuroscience
Eli Lilly

Early in Anne's career, she had the full suite of 4 Jobs: managing a new product launch for a cancer medicine, raising two young children, overseeing a busy household, and caring for her mother, who had Alzheimer's.

The stress of 4 Jobs was buffered by the fact that her husband of 31 years shared household responsibilities equally. He, too, was a busy executive—first a Vice President of Sales for a chemical company and later the owner of a Subway franchise. In their off hours, the couple handles tasks they prefer (he likes, for example, grocery shopping and laundry, and she always took on homework help and scheduling doctors and household repairs). Through the years they usually had someone clean their house every two to four weeks, which, along with daycare, was about the sum of their outsourcing. In retrospect, Anne says they should have outsourced more.

Though Anne has never taken more than a maternity leave, she has made room for lots of fun with her family. They have visited more than 15 countries together—and they love Ireland, especially, where lots of relatives reside. The family also enjoys camping and hiking trips and volunteering together at local Indianapolis charities. A shared appreciation of art draws Anne and her son to classes at a local art school.

In her personal time, Anne enjoys boot camp exercise classes and taking the family dog on long walks. She loves to read, especially biographies of strong women in leadership.

In the category of "the apple doesn't fall far from the tree," Anne's children, 26-year-old fraternal twins, have also chosen careers that fight disease. Her son works for a nonprofit that helps underserved populations manage cancer, and her daughter is pursuing an MD/PhD degree in cancer research at the Indiana University School of Medicine.

Dana White
Dana White, Senior Managing Director
Global Strategic Advisory Practice
Ankura Consulting Group
Former Chief Communications Officer
Hyundai Motor North America

Since Dana was in her mid-30s, she has been her mother's primary caregiver and companion. The time and attention required for this job is like raising children, but often less predictable.

With high-level careers in both government and corporate America, Dana has been able to focus on her work with the help of trusted caregivers. She has hired nurses and aides who fill in for her while she is at work, and that coverage has been invaluable. After one trip with Secretary Mattis, when she was Chief Pentagon Spokesperson, she needed to rush off the plane and go straight to the rehabilitation center where her mother had landed after two falls.

After these two falls, her mother never regained her mobility, and Dana moved her to an assisted living facility close to where she lives. Now she sees her mother several times during the week and spends Sundays with her—always on top of her health and daily needs.

As a longtime caregiver, Dana has made a big effort to carve out time for herself. She rises early and spends at least 30 minutes praying and reading the Bible. She saves Pilates for the evenings, on nights when she is not having dinner with her mom. A lifelong learner, she is taking French lessons twice a week. To unwind completely, she loves a true-crime show, anything on World War II, or an episode of *The Golden Girls*.

As a single woman, Dana keeps her own home running with a full-time housekeeper who has been with her for more than a decade. This woman not only keeps Dana's home in order, but she also provides invaluable eldercare support when Dana is out of town or in busy work periods.

Jonita Wilson
Chief Diversity and Social Impact Officer
Discover Financial Services

At home in Illinois, Jonita and her husband of 29 years (a technology executive) share household responsibilities on an ebb and flow basis. Some weeks the division of labor could be fifty-fifty—or depending on who has a more packed work agenda, the ratio could be seventy-thirty or sixty-forty. Whatever the ratio, they have a give-and-take approach.

Earlier in Jonita's career, when the expense took a chunk out of her smaller paycheck, she still hired a housecleaner in addition to the responsibilities she and her husband covered. This helped to maintain balance in their chaotic household.

When their children were young, the couple relied on daycare facilities. This worked well for the couple's schedule, and they shared the drop-offs and pickups.

As Jonita and her husband raised their children, the family enjoyed traveling, sports events, and trying new restaurants. On her own, Jonita unwinds by watching college football, reading, listening to music/podcasts, taking Zumba and bootcamp classes, going to the movies, and watching reality TV.

Now young adults, their two sons are on the educational path to becoming doctors, and their daughter has a career with the US government.

Jacky Wright
Chief Technology and Platform Officer
McKinsey & Company

Jacky is a UK-born empty nester who splits her time between Florida and London. As a lifelong technologist in a field where women were not in abundance, she had few role models she could turn to for guidance. She forged her path through good judgment, a realistic attitude, and a lot of trial and error.

Starting a family relatively early in her career and having been married twice, Jacky has found the mastery of integrating work and home to be an evolution. In the first phase it was necessary to put her children in daycare at a very early age to accommodate two working parents.

After divorcing, Jacky found that being a single mother meant sometimes having latchkey moments. Asking to leave early to pick up her children from school took courage and an over-functioning work ethic to compensate. In hindsight, working at all hours sometimes took away from effective parenting.

Going into a second marriage and expanding her family, Jacky brought along her lessons learned and an open attitude toward a different approach. That included having intentional conversations about childcare so she could continue to pursue her career in earnest. Were chores always split evenly? Definitely not. Jacky experienced the expectation that mothers bear the brunt of home responsibilities, along with caregiving. Eventually, Jacky's caregiving extended to an aging parent, which required a cross-country move and a job change.

Needless to say, having a huge global role and traveling extensively came at a price. Jacky was not able to attend every school event, and there were many times when it was difficult for her family to see her run for another plane. But, in the end, Jacky has provided a strong foundation for her family, been a solid role model for her three children, and cultivated family relationships based on love and respect whether she is at home or at work.

Nora Zimmett
President, News and Original Series
Weather Group

When Nora is not focused on the weather news, she shares a passion for horseback riding and competitive showing with her 15-year-old daughter—traveling around the United States on the hunter/jumper "AA" circuit. Married for 20 years, her husband is an attorney who has always equally shared household and family responsibilities.

Nora is also active in the animal rights community as a volunteer and supporter of the nonprofit Best Friends Animal Society. She supports the organization's mission to create a better world by advocating for kind and humane treatment of animals. She is also a nationally ranked equestrian and a blogger for *The Chronicle of the Horse*, a monthly Equestrian publication.

Chapter 1

Plan Work and Life From
Your Heart

- Create a life operating model.
- Include some no's in your personal life vision.
- Leave room to let your life flow.
- Get your life before you get a partner.
- Make sure your partner supports your work-life plans.
- Put early deposits in the goodwill bank.
- Don't lose sight of your North Star.

IN MY SENIOR YEAR AT Wheaton College in Massachusetts (when it was still a women's college), my classmates and I were energized by Gloria Steinem's campus visit. When she spoke, she gave us all a big jolt of permission and passion to "have it all"—both work and family.

That all sounded good until years later when many of us were trying to balance work with children and feeling pulled in two very strong directions. Then many women chose to revise Gloria's words to "you can have it all, but not at the same time"—suggesting there had to be periods in and out of the workforce.

That argument's fatal flaw? Most women need to find a reasonable way to stay in the workforce—finding some kind of work that fits life at every age and family stage—to ensure against what I call life's "you never knows" and keep on track for long-term financial security.

As a career coach, I hear lots of sad stories about women suddenly in a perilous financial situation due to an unforeseen divorce—or the job loss, illness, or death of a breadwinning spouse or partner. Though many successfully navigate their way back to jobs they chose to leave behind, it often takes a few years at least to ramp up salaries they need for house mortgages and all essential family needs.

If I had the chance to write speeches for Gloria Steinem today, I would ask her to modify her long-ago proclamation to "You can have it all, as long as you plan ahead." Or, as I say in the introduction, I would put the emphasis on planning ahead so that you can *care for it all.* Long-term financial security calls for nurturing four very important jobs.

Women are by nature caregivers, and aside from demanding professional jobs they often care for children and aging parents—sometimes at the same time. Professions they choose at a young age do not always leave space for evolving caregiving roles. Even as remote work becomes more common in the workplace, it will not change the work lives of most healthcare professionals, for example. Investment bankers still are pretty much tied to their desks. One of my coaching clients, a scientist, can't conduct experiments in a makeshift lab at home.

But this doesn't mean women should not pursue more traditional, workplace-based professions. It means that you should think through several career options and scenarios so you're not surprised years later that you've chosen a profession with little chance of flexibility. If you're a scientist or doctor, think today about things you could do down the road, and tweak your current job description to set yourself up for an adjacent career that will be more flexible and research based. Or if you're an investment banker, develop a network of people who have left Wall Street to start boutique firms that often need part-time help to execute deals.

First and foremost, make sure you're on the same page with your spouse or partner about key issues we all inevitably face. Avoid finding out in the eleventh hour that you're not in agreement about working motherhood, paying for childcare, the kind of childcare you would want, if your two sets of parents will need financial help, and how you and your siblings will handle eldercare. All these things are hot-wire issues that often unnecessarily pit our work against our lives.

Work and family can indeed coexist, and for most women the dual path is both prudent and fulfilling. It's the planning that makes it possible to continually nurture your heart and your mind, and the women quoted in this chapter suggest ways to chart your journey.

Create a life operating model.

To keep her eye on what is most important to her in work and life, Chandra Dhandapani, former Chief Executive Officer of the commercial real estate giant CBRE's Global Workplace Solutions business, created six rules to live by:

- Always respect the individual.
- Keep it simple.
- Keenly prioritize.
- Maintain a healthy balance.
- Learn continuously.
- Don't take yourself too seriously.

She keeps a copy of this list at home and in the office—and these six guidelines she set for herself are always front and center in her mind. When it comes to maintaining a healthy balance, for example, she tries to make sure that work, family, and self-care are relatively equal.

Chandra exercises at least five times a week, unwinds by making dinner for her family almost every night, and lets her family know when she will be in busy periods at work. "To manage expectations, I'll say that for the next three weeks I'll have to work long hours. But I also try to plan for and focus on what we will do as a family when the busy period subsides."

Include some no's in your personal life vision.

When Jill Penrose, Chief People and Company Services Officer of The J.M. Smucker Company, wrote her personal life vision, she had two simple objectives: raise healthy and happy boys and become an officer of her company.

Though getting to the officer level required a lot of hard work, she was never looking to be a hero.

"You don't have to so aggressively lean in that you sacrifice the chance to be a healthy and thriving individual. You don't have to say yes to every task or opportunity. In fact, it's okay to say no in support of other parts of your life."

Leave room to let your life flow.

Professional women often try to control their destiny, but *overplanning* isn't necessarily productive. Young women often ask Janet Foutty, former US Board Chair of Deloitte, which professional level is the best time to start a family. She tells them you can't map it out that carefully—life will flow from what you feel is right in your heart and what's right for your family.

Similarly, Janet advises young women to be open to and curious about many life chapters—but to focus the most on the chapter they're in. "Life takes many unexpected twists and turns that no amount of planning can control. Be present and enjoy your time now. Make the current chapter as productive and fulfilling as possible."

Get your life before you get a partner.

This was advice that Patricia L. Lewis, Chief Sustainability Officer of UnitedHealth Group, often heard from her mother, who believed in establishing a career and having many life experiences before settling down into marriage and starting a family.

Patricia heeded this advice, taking jobs in many areas of the country, working at several different companies, seeing the world, and generally taking a lot of time to build a foundation for herself. She got married at 37 and had her son at 39.

"There are, of course, many more experiences I'll share with my wife and our children, but I'll never have any regrets about first learning and growing on my own."

Make sure your partner supports your work-life plans.

Before you enter a life partnership, it's important to know how your significant other feels about blending work and life. Three questions are particularly important if you someday want to be a mother: Does this person want children? Would this person be okay if you both work while raising a family? Would you or your prospective partner consider a less demanding, more flexible career in order to give one parent more time to take the lead on caregiving?

These initial work–life planning questions determine if you and your partner will be on the same page. But then there is the more nitty-gritty planning that prepares you for starting a family. In my own case, I decided to leave my full-time job early in my marriage to start a marketing consulting firm. My husband knew from the beginning that I had an entrepreneurial bug, and recognized I could have lean income years while I was building a business. I launched my business years before the birth of our first daughter—planning and slowly building the foundation for flexible work I could always do while raising a family.

For Tonit Calaway, Chief Administrative Officer of BorgWarner, "planning" is also her M.O. Before marriage, her husband supported her decision to never give up her job for motherhood. "We had many discussions about the importance of my career and the fact that we would need outside caregiving. We agreed we would find a great daycare facility. My husband knew my approach to caregiving would be as buttoned-up as my advance planning approach to business."

After she got married, but still years before Tonit wanted to start a family, she researched all the daycare facilities in her area. She chose one she felt was best and kept visiting for two years before she was even pregnant. When it was time for her eldest child to go to daycare, she was a well-known face at the center, and the family didn't have any trouble getting a highly coveted spot.

Put early deposits in the goodwill bank.

Part of planning ahead is making work+life investments in your career. When you're less encumbered, Linda Rutherford, Chief Administration Officer of Southwest Airlines, says it's the time to put deposits in the goodwill bank.

"This means going the extra mile with your job—not only to get ahead, but also to establish a bank of trust. With this, leadership is confident and more willing to grant you the flexibility you need when you need to throttle back." Linda admits this can feel like a double standard, but she says we all go above and beyond to hopefully see a return on our investments.

Don't lose sight of your North Star.

All the planning in the world can be for naught if you veer away from your own work+life compass.

Jill Timm, Chief Financial Officer of Kohl's, has an older sister who has a mental disability. Doctors said she would stay at a sixth-grade level and never be able to live or work independently. Her parents chose not to believe that and gave Jill's sister the confidence and support to excel.

"I've always admired my sister who faced and overcame so many challenges. She had a much harder road and she prevailed. In comparison I always had all the tools I needed to succeed. On days when it has been difficult to blend work and life, I've thought of my sister and persevered."

Chapter 2

Create a Real Partnership
with Your Life Partner

- Recognize it takes more than love.
- Figure out who works to live and who lives to work.
- Invest time in your relationship.
- Establish early guidelines for a true partnership.
- Share household responsibilities logically.
- Don't downplay the partner who takes the lead at home.
- Aim for a collegial relationship if your marriage ends in divorce.

A S A CAREER COACH, I see clearly the two sides of having a busy career: on the one hand, work enriches and funds life, though work can get in the way of enjoying that enriched life. But even stay-at-home moms I know find it difficult to fit all the family and household tasks demanding attention in one 24-hour day.

The unfortunate truth is that most women still shoulder most family and household responsibilities. Though men have generally taken on more childcare and household responsibilities than their fathers did, even breadwinning women who outearn their spouses continue to carry the burden of 4 Jobs.[1]

In her book *Fair Play*,[2] Eve Rodsky decided to shine light on the missing "partnership" in the term "life partner." Eve created a system to help couples share all family and household responsibilities more equitably. No one gets off the hook because of big jobs or frequent travel. Everyone has to find a fair way to share the burden and have time left over for self-care and their own definition of fun.

Because women so often leave the workforce when they think things at home are out of control, I became certified as a Fair Play facilitator to help women—and couples—divvy up and *own* various tasks. When women feel they have an equitable partnership with a spouse or partner (with or without additional outside help), they're more likely to stay in the workforce. If they feel they're left alone to spin all the plates in the air, their professional job is the first to go.

While the Fair Play system involves 100 task cards that couples can discuss and divide, even a baby step focusing on a few key responsibilities can start the ball rolling. In many of my conversations with couples, frustrations center around the basics of food (how it gets into the house and onto the table), laundry, and general upkeep of living areas. Few people have someone to help them clean, cook, and do laundry every day—so many of these tasks default to an overworked mother.

Since these tasks can be both annoying and difficult, couples find that once they really focus on what each task entails and who is more suited to own the responsibility, simple solutions emerge.

You can create more harmony in your daily living and a true foundation of sharing (even if it's not exactly fifty-fifty!). There are endless ways to divvy up responsibilities...but not doing so at all is the one way to cause underlying strife. As evidenced by the wisdom in this chapter, tackling and finding solutions for what Eve calls "the daily grind" gives you the bandwidth to strengthen all aspects of your partnership.

Recognize it takes more than love.

Sharon Ryan, the former General Counsel of International Paper, has been happily married for more than 30 years, and she credits the longevity to a true partnership commitment.

"Sure, my husband and I love each other very much, but when we were both working, it took more than just love to make it through the craziness of every day. We talked a lot about what is important to us as a couple, what we want for our family, how we could both get the 'me time' we needed, and how our household could generally run more smoothly—and what we each needed to do as partners to reach those goals. And we were honest about the fact that during certain busy work or life periods we might not have as much time for each other…but we planned how to make up for it later."

Figure out who works to live and who lives to work.

In Linda Rutherford's marriage, she is the partner who lives to work. Before her husband retired, he worked to live.

Their basic attitudes toward work shaped the way they divided household responsibilities. Her husband has often taken on more household tasks to make it possible for Linda to keep growing in her career—and reach her position of Chief Administration Officer at Southwest Airlines.

Generally speaking, though, the couple considers their marriage a merger of equals. They work hard to avoid unfair burdens and aim to be strong and participative partners. Part of their strategy is to play to each other's strengths. Linda is responsible for tasks such as making sure the house is clean, keeping their social calendar, gift buying, and decorating—while her husband takes the lead on cooking, laundry, and all house maintenance.

Invest time in your relationship.

There's a phase in many families when every minute of the day seems to revolve around kids. Jennifer Piepszak, the Co-Chief Executive Officer of the Commercial and Investment Bank at JPMorganChase remembers that when their kids were young, her husband would occasionally go on work trips with her so they could spend more time together.

The couple also managed to fit in date nights here and there and focused on the fact that "this all started with you." (They started dating at age 17.) "And if we do it right, it will end with you, too."

Establish early guidelines for a true partnership.

"Start as you intend to continue" is advice from Anne White, President of Eli Lilly Neuroscience. "Get away from the idea early on that one parent is the leader and the other is the helper. You are Co-CEOs of the household."

Red flags: you're doing all the housework or all the cooking and cleanup. "You want to be with someone who doesn't need to be asked and just pitches in as a matter of course. But at the same time, don't expect your spouse to be a mind reader. If you really need help, you need to say it."

This was a lesson Jordana Kammerud, Chief Human Resources Officer at Corning, had to learn. It's not that her husband didn't help, it's that they never had the conversation about divvying up responsibilities in ways that made sense based on schedules and availability.

"Instead of saying, here's how you can help me, I waited until I was angry to say he should be doing this or that, which was not fair to either of us."

Once they had the conversation, Jordana's husband didn't have to guess about which household and family tasks he should do, and she saw many things migrate off her to-do list. "We were both happier and in household-chore harmony."

Anne also believes distinct responsibilities are key. "You're both busy; you both have important jobs." Her husband's career was in chemical sales with a lot of travel. He took the lead on cooking, grocery shopping, and laundry. She took most of the school-related responsibilities, including volunteering and parent-teacher conferences.

"My biggest piece of advice once responsibilities are divided: don't micromanage. I say it's fine that things are done his way."

Then Anne says, get out of the house, get away for a dinner or a walk, and talk about how things are working. "Treat household management like a business relationship. Keep it professional, not emotional, by reflecting on how things are going rather than reacting in the moment."

Share household responsibilities logically.

Household harmony does not necessarily mean a fifty-fifty division of labor. Just like there is no perfect work–life "balance," Beautycounter Founder Gregg Renfrew believes that sharing household responsibilities with your partner can't always be even.

Without a doubt, Gregg says your partner should alleviate the burden. "It can't always be a perfect division of labor, but don't let everything rest on your shoulders."

Ultimately, two people are aiming for a strong life partnership while leading very busy lives. Jill Penrose, Chief People and Company Services Officer at The J.M. Smucker Co., always chose to "assume good intent," knowing there would be logical times when one person is leading and the other is supporting.

Don't downplay the partner who takes the lead at home.

A CEO I once interviewed told me she always advises young women to discuss if she or her partner will take the lead on earning the household income—before they enter a long-term relationship. She called it "the business side" of a marriage or partnership.

In many relationships, an imbalance in earnings can create tension—
or even blows to ego. A practical conversation from financial, relationship, and psychological standpoints can avoid any difficulties.

This is especially true when traditional roles are reversed, and it is the
husband who takes the lead at home. U.S. Steel's Chief Financial Officer
Jessica Graziano's husband was initially in the insurance industry and then
became a professor and mental health counselor. She was the busy corporate executive, and her husband had more flexibility to run the household.

Though her husband enjoyed the second careers that he chose, his
traditional male ego suffered a bit knowing his wife was the major breadwinner. To ensure that his self-worth was totally intact, Jessica told him
he was not only her husband and coparent, but he was also her professional colleague making it possible for her to earn her salary and support
their family. "I said repeatedly I could not do any of it without his support. It's not my money, it's our money—and together we are successful."

Aim for a collegial relationship if your marriage ends in divorce.

When Suzanne Powers, the former Global Chief Product Officer of
McCann Worldgroup, divorced her first husband, she did not divorce the
family unit they created. Every Sunday the divorced couple and their two
sons continue to have a family dinner.

The advertising executive, who has now launched her own firm, Powers Creativity, says, "We never let the divorce get in the way of the family's needs. We put aside our annoyances and avoided putting the kids in
the middle of our differences. My ex-husband is the father of my children
and that will never change."

A collegial relationship makes it easier to co-parent. Once Suzanne was
on a plane to Los Angeles when one son badly broke his leg. "Because we
really made an effort to continue our relationship and work together, we've
handled both the crises and the day-to-day challenges more smoothly."

Chapter 3

Be True to Your Professional DNA

- Remember what makes you tick.
- Know what you need to be your best self.
- Tell your kids you have more than one job.
- Know if you love your work, you won't regret your work.
- Let your true self be visible.

THROUGH THE YEARS, I'VE VOLUNTEERED for various school and community organizations, and in every case, I worked alongside impressive ex-corporate women who left the workforce to care for their families. As volunteers they ran meetings with no-nonsense military precision, and after one particularly strident "you-better-be-on-your-toes" missive the nonprofit's executive director leaned over to me and said, "We've got to get women like this back to corporate America."

School and nonprofit organizations certainly benefit from the business experience of women on hiatus from the workforce, yet their energies often outpace the typical fundraising event. From my coaching practice I know that many of these women feel stuck between a rock and a hard place: they didn't really want to leave the workforce, and they also felt they needed to spend more time at home. But they are wired for high-energy careers and feel a mounting sense of frustration as stay-at-home mom years add up.

The bottom line is that you know who you are. You know if you want and need the stimulation of a professional career, and you know if you're completely satisfied raising a family, running a household, and volunteering in your community. My observation is that too many women who really enjoy their professional careers leave the workforce prematurely, without fully exploring options other than rigid full-time, in-the-office roles.

It does not have to be a binary work or no-work choice—and work does not need to alienate your family. One C-suite woman who sadly passed away before this book was published told me she had found ways to find joy in both her work and her family at every life stage. She chose not to put off work experiences "for another time"—from the start of her career she embraced a wide range of opportunities—living and working in many countries and eventually exposing her family to many different cultures.

Though many would prefer to stay closer to home, this woman also found simple ways to connect her son to her work—bringing him to company events and seating him in the audience during her big presentations. She made sure she was at all her son's major school events, and when she couldn't be at a less important event, she simply—and honestly—explained why.

From a very young age her son admired her accomplishments, and he knew early on that work was part of what made his mother who she was. When she was diagnosed with a terminal illness, she felt the unfairness of the situation, but she did not feel regret. She knew she had followed her true passions, achieved major goals, and fully nurtured both her career and her family every step of the way.

"No regrets" is a universal theme I found with all the women who commented in this chapter and the book overall.

Remember what makes you tick.

Tonit Calaway, Chief Administrative Officer of BorgWarner, has always been a caring and involved mother, but also a mother who unapologetically has let her children and others in her life know she also cares very much for her career. Avoiding work-versus-home waffling, she has shown her daughter and son (now an actress and a student at an Ivy League university) she is happy and passionate about her work. Viewing this passion, resolve, and commitment, her children have always accepted and supported her work as "This is a big part of what makes our mom the good mom that she is."

Similarly, Vonage Chief Marketing Officer and Head of Integration Joy Corso reminds herself and others to do all the things that give you fulfillment. "Strive to be your whole person. Being a good mom, and spending time with family and friends are a big part of that fulfillment. But working hard and having professional success are also fulfilling for me and others. Don't feel guilty about pursuing your own passions and fulfillment, because without them you'll never feel like a whole person."

Eli Lilly Neuroscience President Anne White also will not give in to guilt and worry about working. "Don't assume your kids will feel neglected or resentful. If you show them you're doing important work they can relate to, they'll be interested and proud."

Anne's kids came by the office frequently, and for a while they even had their own office—a vacant one next to hers. For her employer at the time, a pharmaceutical start-up, they drew ads for fictitious medicines.

"I always told my twins I help people by helping the company develop new cancer and Alzheimer's medicines." This hit home: two of their grandparents died of cancer, and one of Alzheimer's. It then all came full circle: her daughter is now in cancer research and her son works for a nonprofit that helps cancer patients with life needs.

Some may say it's easier to show kids you're helping people in an obvious helping profession. That's true, but even if you're a banker, for example, you're helping people save enough money to send their kids to college.

Know what you need to be your best self.

Ocean Spray Chief Commercial Officer Monisha Dabek knows some women just aren't cut out to be stay-at-home mothers.

"I've been a better mom because I allowed myself to have the career I fundamentally needed to thrive. Everyone doesn't need that professional outlet, but I let myself say I'm not wired to stay home. I needed more variety to stay sane—and because I've been honest with myself, I've never lost who I am."

Jonita Wilson, Chief Diversity and Social Impact Officer at Discover Financial Services, echoes the need to be true to yourself. It was always her goal to strive for a successful career. Of course, she wanted to be a good mom, but she also never wanted to leave the workforce. "I see working as a personal freedom and a form of self-care. I knew I didn't want to buck up against the life I truly wanted."

Tell your kids you have more than one job.

"I've always told my kids I have multiple jobs: their mother, dad's wife, and Founder of Beautycounter," says Gregg Renfrew.

So her kids would never feel her work was totally separate from them, she found ways to bring them into the fold—they participated in company events, tested new products, and saw how she used Beautycounter products at home.

Gregg believes that if kids know, unequivocally, they can always reach you, your time away from family is easier to accept. "When one of my kids calls me at work, I always answer—usually whatever they need can be satisfied in 30 quick seconds. As women, we need to stop apologizing for having a life outside of the home."

Know if you love your work, you won't regret your work.

The reality that no working mother has it all figured out is a comfort to one Chief Executive Officer in the beauty industry. Like every other mother she has her moments of doubt about whether she is doing enough for her child.

The panacea for doubt and guilt, she says, is the simple question "Do I love the work I do?" She believes this is a critical question when women are at a breaking point and feel they need to leave the workforce. They may need to leave a job they don't love—not the workforce altogether.

"If you love your job—if it's more than a paycheck—and it enriches your life, it's easier to make trade-offs and sacrifices and endure the particularly busy days or weeks when you feel pulled in too many directions. And it's easier not to regret your choices and throw in the towel if you know your work represents your passions and who you are."

Let your true self be visible.

When UnitedHealth Group Chief Sustainability Officer Patricia L. Lewis was midway through her career, she came out to her professional colleagues. She felt an obligation to share her story with others in the LGBTQ+ community—who often feel isolated and invisible.

"Hearing an African American woman at the management level be open and honest helped others speak up about their own identities. Bring your authentic self to work and talk openly about your life and your family. When you don't have to hide, you have the freedom to be your best self and do your best work."

Chapter 4

Tune Out Naysayers Who Judge Your Career Decisions

- Ignore judgments from friends and family.
- Make your own work and life choices and stand firm.
- Know you're damned if you do, and damned if you don't.
- Find a middle ground that lessens motherhood guilt.
- Get the semantics right: others help *you* raise your children.
- Realize that the "motherhood and apple pie" theory can be half-baked.
- Don't let stereotypes rule your family.
- Set your own standards for successful working motherhood.
- Be realistic: any life choice could lead to regrets.
- Live and let live.
- Remember that working is a woman's fundamental right.

EVERYBODY HAS AN OPINION ABOUT working motherhood. In my experience as a career coach, I can confirm that the age-old work-versus-stay-home debate is alive and well. The U.S. Department of Labor reports that about 45% of women were unemployed in the March 2021 to March 2024 time period,[1] and women often cite the cost and scarcity of childcare as the reason they have stayed home.

Interestingly, though, I still encounter many young mothers who tell me they simply believe it is best to be 100 percent focused on home and family—despite any current or future financial needs. When I continue to peel the onion, I often find out that a mother, mother-in-law, sister, or group of friends has proclaimed only one "right" way to raise children.

Those holding this view imply that working motherhood is detrimental to children. Prominent researchers have debunked this theory, including those who conducted a Harvard Business School study and concluded that maternal employment does not affect kids' happiness in adulthood. For daughters, especially, working mothers provide an advantage: across two multinational datasets spanning 29 countries and two decades, researchers found that adult daughters of employed moms are more likely to work, to be supervisors, and to earn higher wages than daughters of mothers who stayed at home full time. The effects remained, even after controlling for parents' education and type of employment.[2]

So, the right way to raise children is the way *you* truly believe is right and the way *you* unapologetically own. Today it's much easier to own the working mother path. Well before "remote work" was a trend, I moved from a traditional full-time, in-the-office role to a consulting practice I operated out of my home, then to two different businesses I launched with partners—both hybrid work arrangements, and then back to a career-coaching business in a home office. In each of these flexible work scenarios, I ignored those who questioned my choices and focused on being a fully present professional and a fully present mom—building an interesting resume, rarely missing a school event, and logging many carpooling miles.

All women I interviewed for this book faced naysayers at some point in their careers, but as noted in their tips in this chapter, they found a way to stay true to themselves, tune out the noise, and carry on.

Ignore judgments from friends and family.

While Southwest Airlines Chief Administration Officer Linda Rutherford's children were young, many people tried to tell her there was one right way to tackle each aspect of child-rearing.

"There is no right and wrong—no one perfect answer. There is only what is right for your family."

And "family" refers to the parents and children family unit that lives under your roof.

Regeneron Pharmaceuticals Chief Diversity, Equity and Inclusion Officer Smita Pillai has experienced many judgments from family living thousands of miles away. She grew up in a very traditional family in India. Even during a recent visit to her home country, all of her relatives spoke enthusiastically to her husband about his work, and then turned to her and said, "Are you still working? Don't you think you should be home with your children?"

One of Smita's children has always been challenging, and some family members attribute it to the fact that she's a working mother who hasn't spent enough time with the child. Smita knows that her strong-willed child isn't acting out for lack of mothering; it is just her personality.

"When you're in the judgment line of fire, tell yourself you're doing the absolute best you can do as a mother. You don't need anyone's approval to keep working."

Jill Timm, the Kohl's Chief Financial Officer, grew up in a very traditional American household where her mother did not work and always had dinner on the table at 5:00 p.m. Though it was a generation later, her mother did not understand Jill's decision to work after her first child was born, and she went so far as to say, "I hope it's worth it."

Jill made it known that the comment was hurtful, but she also knew her parents were both very supportive in helping her take care of her daughters. Her mother also couldn't understand why Jill would want to put her kids in daycare but became a believer when the teachers detected her younger daughter's speech issue very early on. Her mother said she wouldn't have known there was a problem, and she visited the daycare center and saw her granddaughters were very happy, and the center was high quality and well run.

Make your own work and life choices and stand firm.

U.S. Steel Chief Financial Officer Jessica Graziano made peace with the fact that her family did not fit the traditional mold.

She chose not to listen to the naysayers who questioned her choice to work and learned to ignore snarky comments like, "You have to travel... again?" Instead, she maintained her positive outlook, knowing her kids were good people with good friends and excellent grades—not in any way disadvantaged by her professional career.

"In the early days I would try to make excuses about a 10-day business trip to Hong Kong or South Africa. Then I stood firmly in my choices and simply took the attitude that it is what it is."

Know you're damned if you do, and damned if you don't.

Jacinth Smiley agrees that you should make your best decisions about work and life, and then don't apologize or get trapped in mommy guilt. With pragmatism the Hormel Foods Chief Financial Officer says, "You will always be damned if you do or damned if you don't—there are judgments on all sides of the work/don't work issue. Be purposeful and make time for the things that really matter to your family."

Knowing this can be easier said than done, she adds, "Believe in the bond you have with your family and don't continually second-guess your decisions."

Find a middle ground that lessens motherhood guilt.

When Ally Financial Chief Audit Executive Stephanie Richard's children were young, they would sadly watch her go on business trips or lament the fact that she didn't pick them up from school—and they would say they wished she was a stay-at-home mom.

"Rather than letting myself spiral down into the abyss of guilt, I would tell them this is who I am. I love my family and I love my work. Both make me the person who I am, and both make me your mom. I would also tell them if I were to stay home I would most likely be a Helicopter Mom—and weren't they lucky to have much more independence?!"

Stephanie also realized that compromises could go a long way. "When I was at the manager/director level, I rearranged my schedule so I could leave the office early on Fridays and my kids looked forward to seeing me at the school pickup that day."

Get the semantics right: others help YOU raise your children.

When Mary Mack was early in her career, her mother asked, "Does it bother you that someone else is raising your children?"

But Mary, who retired as Chief Executive Officer of Consumer and Small Business Banking at Wells Fargo, never let this misperception bother her. Her family had the same nanny in their lives for 25 years, and she loved Mary's children like her own. Mary firmly knew the nanny was *helping* her raise her children.

Realize that the "motherhood and apple pie" theory can be half-baked.

After being raised in India, Mastercard's Chief Commercial Payments Officer Raj Seshadri is often perplexed by American society's angst over women working versus always being home taking care of their kids. In her native India, many traditional women don't work but it's expected and accepted that good and caring mothers will have babysitters, family, and friends pitching in as a broader community to care for and raise your children.

"Independence and family connection are not mutually exclusive."

Don't let stereotypes rule your family.

Raj also believes that it doesn't make sense to hold fast to traditional family stereotypes found in any culture. The father in her household, for example, is in an equally demanding job, and he is actually the cook and a better baker.

During the pandemic when the entire family was home, Raj's teenage sons would come downstairs asking "What's for dinner?" They were soon assigned a night they were responsible for cooking—dismissing the idea that only a mother or a parent can prepare meals.

"In our family, we promote the idea that anyone can do anything."

Set your own standards for successful working motherhood.

The Weather Group's President of News and Original Series Nora Zimmett admits she is not the mother who has a color-coded calendar tracking work and family events.

"I can't bake brownies—even out of a box. I'm not great at all the day-to-day details, and I don't know half the teachers' names. But fortunately, my husband is a true male feminist and fifty-fifty partner. Between us—and with the help of a nanny—we keep our daughter safe, happy, and where she needs to be. It's not always perfect—and I would never be seen as the stereotypical mother and homemaker—but we've created a life that gives each of us room to flourish and grow."

Be realistic: any life choice could lead to regrets.

Edward Jones Managing Partner Penny Pennington encourages women to work hard to get rid of their mom guilt, because she believes no life choice is without a few regrets. The feeling that you *should* be home with your children 24/7 plagues many working mothers, but Penny says you have to consciously work through it mentally, spiritually, and physically.

Various morning and evening routines continually ground her in her work and life decisions. Just seven minutes of meditation in the morning calms her mind. Every evening before bed she has one hour of alone time when she usually reads about art.

"Even if I had chosen not to work, there would still be guilt and regrets. It's natural to question your choices from time to time, but you can't give the what-ifs too much space in your mind."

Live and let live.

The Founder of Beautycounter, Gregg Renfrew, hopes fewer women will judge the decisions other women make, especially when it comes to work and family.

"Allow women to live their lives as they see fit. Lift them up rather than passing judgment. Be at peace with the decisions you've made for yourself and your family. Don't look for validation from other people—just be confident in yourself."

Remember that working is a woman's fundamental right.

When Raj Seshadri was growing up, her mother broke through traditional stereotypes in India— earning three degrees and becoming an educator after her children started school.

"My mother's mantra was that women have the fundamental right to learn, work, and earn. All women should feel comfortable exercising that right and working toward economic equality."

Chapter 5

Don't Hide the Fact You're a Mother

- Work for a company that supports life.
- Look beyond politically correct messaging.
- Bring your whole self to the office.
- Blur the lines between work and home.
- Reveal the human side of your professional persona.
- Remember that the people who matter aren't keeping score.
- Talk openly about your real-life issues.

GONE ARE THE DAYS WHEN mothers had to sneak out of the office to get to a soccer game or school concert. Even the largest, most bureaucratic corporations have finally realized the lives of their employees do not revolve solely around their paid professions.

Flexibility is now more the rule than the exception. Corporate leaders are not acting solely from the goodness of their hearts—they know that flexible work drives revenue growth. One study conducted in partnership with Boston Consulting Group found when the average public company lets employees decide whether to come into the office it sees revenue growth that outperforms others by 16 percentage points.[1]

This data is a very compelling reason why most companies have loosened traditional work structures. Sixty-nine percent of all United States companies now offer some degree of workplace location flexibility for corporate employees. Within that statistic 32 percent of companies are fully flexible (either operating with a fully remote workforce or giving employees a choice of where they want to work), and 37% offer a structured hybrid arrangement (alternating days in the office with remote work).[2]

Greater work flexibility is great, but that does not necessarily mean women see it as license to reveal their work-life struggle. Though the pandemic literally brought children front and center (on many a Zoom call screen), many women still feel they need to downplay their motherhood role to get ahead.

Thankfully, this chapter—with advice from women at the very top of the corporate ladder—shows there's no need to hide the fact that you're a mother. It's okay to talk about the struggle, as long as you're smart about trying to find solutions suitable for both you and your employer. Every woman in the workforce has wrestled with some or all the 4 Jobs, and showing vulnerability (rather than false bravado) opens the door to a work arrangement that truly fits your life.

Work for a company that supports life.

Northwestern Mutual's Chief Strategy Officer Aditi Javeri Gokhale has advice for job seekers: look for a company and boss that align with your personal value system. "No amount of money or a lofty title will sustain you if the overall company culture is not the right fit."

During an interview is the best time to have the candid conversation about your responsibilities and needs as a working mother and/or a daughter of aging parents. "Don't be afraid to nix an opportunity. If the company or the boss is not supportive, you don't want that job or that company."

Look beyond politically correct messaging.

How do you get the flexibility you want and need—and the respect you want as a working mother? Edward Jones Managing Partner Penny Pennington says when you're looking for a new employer, you can't simply rely on the "politically correct" website messaging. Make sure the video matches the soundtrack, so you'll be working for a company that truly cares about the health and well-being of its employees.

"Talk to as many people as you can—hopefully you'll be interviewed by more than one person. Then try to talk to others you may know in the company or those who used to work there. Make sure there's consistency in the way everyone talks about the company culture. Listen carefully—culture is how the environment makes you feel."

Bring your whole self to the office.

When Kris Malkoski, the Segment Chief Executive Officer of Learning & Development at Newell Brands, was rising in her career, women had only recently broken through barriers in marketing. She had achieved the Director title, and only about 20 percent of professionals at that level were women.

Despite her rising success, one of her male colleagues said, "Kris, you've got to tone it down a bit with all the pictures of your kids in your office. And you made it so obvious you were leaving the office to go to your daughter's holiday concert. You're making a lot of men on the team uncomfortable, and they're questioning your professional focus."

Kris stood her ground and said her performance proved that her professional focus was fine. Since then, she has encouraged all her colleagues—both men and women—to be more transparent about their families, too.

Without a doubt, working at home during the pandemic brought a lot of children out of hiding. Though Hewlett Packard Enterprise Chief Financial Officer Marie Myers was never one to keep her children in the background, on April Fools' Day during a Zoom call her young daughter literally took center stage. She put on Marie's clothes and started to run the meeting—a performance that Marie did not shut down.

Blur the lines between work and home.

Many women used to be afraid to mention they had children. Mother-hood is not taboo in the business world today, but one Chief Executive Officer in the beauty industry encourages mothers to be very open about commitments to both work and family. "Being an amazing mom and having an amazing career are not mutually exclusive. In fact, they each can make the other stronger."

To make sure her colleagues are comfortable revealing their mul-tifaceted lives, she blurs the lines between her own work and home. "I sometimes bring my son to the office and company events, so he sees the actual people I spend time with every day. At work I talk about my son and my family all the time. It's important that I set an example and always help my team find the space for both work and family—whether they are mothers or fathers, aunts and uncles, sons and daughters, broth-ers and sisters. We all have our own unique situations, and being there for our families is an essential and magical part of life."

Aditi Javeri Gokhale agrees that when you try to keep your work and home lives totally separate, it creates more pressure to always give each equal time. "I consider my team and peers an extension of my family. When you develop trusting, collegial relationships at work, it can also benefit your family. My son enjoys going to work events and considers many of my colleagues his friends, too. When we moved from New York City to Milwaukee during the pandemic, my colleagues helped us find a home. My son knows I'm spending my work hours with people who care about us."

At any level, women can help to bring life to work. Former General Counsel of International Paper Sharon Ryan encouraged her colleagues to contribute to a photo montage of family dogs, what was outside their windows at home, or pictures of them as children. "Showing we all have lives beyond work goes a long way in nurturing a healthy company culture."

Reveal the human side of your professional persona.

Kimberly Paige, Chief Marketing Officer of BET Networks (Black Entertainment Television), has a motto: "I know where I work, but I know who I serve."

This means Kimberly has never been afraid to speak her truth: her family is her priority. At one point, when she was soon to earn the Vice President title, her daughter was transitioning to the difficult middle school years. Kimberly knew her daughter needed more time with her at home.

Rather than leaving the workforce altogether, Kimberly knew even one more day at home could make a big difference. She spoke to her boss about a compressed workweek—fitting her job into four longer days.

"This gave me another full day off my daughter could count on. I was able to spend more time at school, help her navigate tricky middle school friendships, and generally be there when she needed to talk."

The compressed workweek did not adversely affect Kimberly's career progression...and she got the VP job as expected. "In fact, throughout my career, the more human and authentic I was, the more promotions I got."

Remember that the people who matter aren't keeping score.

When you set boundaries for your professional life, they aren't necessarily what others on your team choose for their own lives. As long as your colleagues know you'll always get the work done—and never let your own needs get in their way—you have the freedom to say what work arrangement works best for the rhythm of your life.

Edward Jones Managing Partner Penny Pennington's team knows Friday nights are reserved for date nights with her husband and, barring an emergency, most of Saturday she preserves as family time. Sundays she is generally more focused on getting ready for the upcoming workweek. Though she feels these boundaries are right for her—and, most important, they are sustainable over time—she still feels a twinge of self-doubt when she reads about other executives who are up and at 'em at 4:00 a.m. and available 24/7.

"I just have to let it go and not compare myself to others. What works for me will not necessarily work for someone else—and no one important is keeping score."

Talk openly about your real-life issues.

When former Wells Fargo Chief Executive Officer of Consumer and Small Business Banking Mary Mack's daughter died at age 23, she found herself in a very dark place. Many said CEOs should not talk about tragedies like this...because it somehow made them seem weak. Mary chose instead to openly talk about it and lean into the realities of her family's deeply personal and traumatic experience.

Mary said coming back to work was part of her healing. "Work isn't just about a paycheck; it also nurtures and feeds your life. I wanted to show people how work gives you a reason to muscle through when circumstances make it seem like you should give up. I also wanted others going through unimaginable tragedy to have hope that better is possible."

She encourages others to be transparent too—about life tragedies and everyday challenges. With obvious trepidation a man on her team once said he was leaving early to go to a child's basketball game. Mary said "great," and he replied, "It felt so good to tell you where I was really going, rather than lying about it and feeling guilty."

Chapter 6

Look Before You Leap Out of the Workforce

- Keep an eye on your own financial security.
- Realize there's no perfect time to work.
- Know that bigger kids often have bigger problems.
- Consider if your job is the scapegoat for a difficult time at home.
- Try not to let an emotional low push you out the door.
- Accept that the hardest part of motherhood probably won't be the longest.
- Don't let a situation that will disrupt your life for 30 days derail a career you could have for 30 years.
- If you love what you do, weather the ups and downs.
- Make sure you know and use your company's work–life benefits.
- Face your financial reality and ask for typical and atypical help.
- Find "half answers" for a work–life compromise.
- Explore a part-time schedule with your current employer.
- Realize an entrepreneurial venture can be more work than a corporate job.
- Save valuable family time by shortening your commute.

- Consider leaving the workforce just one of many options.
- If you do take a hiatus, be strategic.
- When you return to work after a hiatus, put your ego aside.
- Consider smaller companies for an easier post-hiatus return.

FROM MY WORK COACHING WOMEN since 2002, my anecdotal data is that women say they'll leave the workforce "for a couple of years to get things at home in order," but they actually stay out for an average of 12. That's because life happens (and happens and happens again), and there never seems to be a good time to go back.

With very few exceptions, though, it's difficult for one salary to cover a lifetime of family expenses. Even those one-income households that can comfortably afford mortgages and all day-to-day expenses can suddenly feel the strain of multiple college tuitions and less-than-robust retirement accounts. Add in possible financial help for up to four aging parents who outlive their money, and the basic math shows women the wisdom of always having a paycheck—no matter the size.

The potential loss of income did not stop two-thirds of women to consider leaving the workforce in 2023 due to the stress and cost of childcare.[1] If you, too, are evaluating whether it's "worth it" to work, remember that the cost of childcare is an investment in your career and salary progression.

The reality is that childcare may cause leaner years of take-home pay, but the financial impact of many years out of the workforce is far greater. The following is the math that most women (and their partners) do not do.

The Center for American Progress uses a moderate-income example: assume a new mother leaves her $50,000/year job to stay home with her baby during five pre-school years. This absence would cost her approximately $250,000 in income, $235,000 in lost wage growth, and $210,000 in retirement assets and benefits over her career lifespan.[2] That's a total loss of approximately $700,000 for a much shorter hiatus than what I have seen as the average. And the loss is obviously greater for women who leave higher-paying jobs.

Compare the $700,000 loss to the cost of childcare for the same five pre-school years. The Care.com 2024 Cost of Care Report ranks a nanny as the most expensive childcare resource at an average cost of $766 per week or $199,160 for five years. A daycare center has an average cost of $321 per week or $83,460 for five years.[3]

Even for the most expensive childcare, the cost of staying out of the workforce is more than three times greater.

My mission is to keep women in the workforce—to avoid huge financial losses that threaten their long-term security. As you will see in this chapter, senior leaders want to help you stay in the workforce, too. Any male holdouts who still have traditional views of how and where work should be done are increasingly drowned out by vocal female leaders. These women know the years you have young children are few, and that giving you the chance to keep working in a flexible way in the short term means they will benefit from your talents in the long term. Before you decide to leave, do the math, know all the ways you could possibly structure your job, and have an open conversation with your boss.

Keep an eye on your own financial security.

When Martine Ferland, former Chief Executive Officer of Mercer (a Marsh McLennan company), advises young women, she stresses the importance of financial independence. Traditionally men were the default breadwinners, but now in same-sex partnerships, one woman can also defer to the other to take all the financial responsibility.

"In any marriage or long-term partnership, though, you need to be able to support yourself and your family in the wake of unforeseen circumstances. Choose a profession you'll like over time and always keep the women's trifecta in mind: we live longer, have more work gaps, and often earn less. As women, we need to cultivate both an emotionally rich and financially sound life."

PPG General Counsel Anne Foulkes calls financial independence the buffer for many life curveballs. After her father disappeared when she was six months old, Anne was raised by a single mother. Not one to be defeated, her mother enrolled in graduate school and became a social worker. "With my mother as an example, I'm realistic about life's twists and turns—and I advise my daughters to always be on steady ground to manage the unexpected."

Shannon Lapierre, the former Chief Communications Officer at Stanley Black & Decker, tells young mothers the struggles during the early career and family years are so important, giving you the foundation to take care of yourself and your family if life takes that unexpected turn. "Persevere, get through it, and recognize those years are few but powerful in terms of career progression and working toward long-term financial security."

Realize there's no perfect time to work.

If women stay home when their children are young, they often think they'll get past their caregiving job and reach a point that makes more sense to work.

Former International Paper General Counsel Sharon Ryan said her caregiving role lasted many years past the toddler stage. With her sisters she managed her mother's end-of-life care, and she subsequently cared for her father before he passed away at age 97 with Alzheimer's. Outside of her family, she was also a caregiver to a close friend who had cancer.

Sharon found the eldercare stage in life much more stressful than the child-rearing years. "With young children life is fairly predictable—with aging parents, you never know when you're going to get that 2 a.m. phone call or need to be talking to doctors for a medical emergency."

Janet Foutty, former US Board Chair of Deloitte, also experienced life's many twists and turns—and various caregiving needs for herself and others. On the same day she got her first national leadership job, she found out she had breast cancer. When she reached another big professional milestone, her daughter was having health issues.

"Life has a way of catching up with you. Be intentional about making your job work for you and your family in all situations. Develop the confidence that you can put everything you need in place. Give yourself a sense of control, knowing you always have accountability and responsibility to yourself, your family, and your colleagues to weather any life storm."

Know that bigger kids often have bigger problems.

There is no life phase when your family needs you most. McKinsey Chief Technology and Platform Officer Jacky Wright says your children need you at every age—and you can continually adjust to fit work around your extended family's evolving circumstances.

Adult children have adult challenges. Though Jacky's kids are all cultivating interesting careers, they sometimes struggle thinking they need to reach her level of success. She advises them to have a rich life, not necessarily a big job or a lot of money. "It takes my time and careful attention to help my older kids shape their lives. We do a lot of soul-searching in discussions about, for example, aiming for the smaller house if that's where you will more easily be a family and spend time together without the worry of too much overhead."

Consider if your job is the scapegoat for a difficult time at home.

U.S. Bancorp's President Gunjan Kedia knew a colleague was going through a rough time with her young daughter. But her colleague talked less about what was going on at home, and more about her "awful job." Though no job is perfect, Gunjan knew this woman took a lot of pride in and enjoyed her work. Regardless, she was going to run away from her job without first trying to figure out the situation with her daughter.

"I tried to help my colleague focus on all the great things about her job and what she could do to alleviate the situation with her daughter. When you're excited about your work, you have more emotional space to solve life's challenges."

Try not to let an emotional low push you out the door.

When Weyerhaeuser Chief Administrative Officer Denise Merle's mother passed away, she had a young family and a demanding job. In her grief she told her sister she just couldn't do both anymore and she would have to leave her job. Her sister sympathized but advised her to wait a year before leaving—noting it was not a time to make a major life decision.

Denise listened... and stuck it out for another 30 years.

A colleague had a similar feeling when her own mother was ill. She came to Denise saying she needed to end her 30-year career to be with her mother. Denise pointed out alternatives to a total departure, suggesting her colleague go on family medical leave for three months.

Another pregnant colleague announced she would leave after her baby was born. She was worried about working full time and said she could only work 30 hours a week. Feeling stressed about blending work and motherhood, she made the snap judgment that a reduced schedule would be impossible. Denise encouraged her to keep an open mind and ask for a new work structure—and the woman not only stayed, but soon earned a promotion.

Accept that the hardest part of motherhood probably won't be the longest.

Young mothers who have children wholly dependent on them often feel overwhelmed by a long list of tasks that must be done right away.

Martine Ferland has always advised working mothers to accept that it's demanding to both work and raise a family. But don't let that keep you from being present in—and enjoying—this moment in time. "It's actually relatively few years before children are more independent, giving you a bit more independence, too."

Martine knows many women can't see the light at the end of the tunnel and think the answer is to leave the workforce when children are very young. While everyone has to make their own decisions, she suggests an alternative is to set boundaries (and it's especially wise to do this at the beginning of a new job). "Know yourself, know how you're wired and what you need to be satisfied in both work and life."

As a high-energy person, the answer for Martine was to work extra hours during the week so she could put firm boundaries around family time on the weekends. "Saturdays and Sundays were big blocks of time when my children could expect my full presence. I also arranged my schedule to be home for family dinner most weeknights and pick up work again when kids were in bed. Boundaries created rituals my family could depend on."

Don't let a situation that will disrupt your life for 30 days derail a career you could have for 30 years.

U.S. Steel Chief Financial Officer Jessica Graziano is often approached by women who have a crisis at home—and their knee-jerk reaction can be to leave the workforce. While she is sympathetic to difficult situations, she also tries to give these colleagues some important perspective.

"Often, we face situations that seem life-changing but will only pose short-term challenges. I encourage women to think through solutions and timelines. They might just need some time off... not a complete hiatus from the workforce."

Similarly, when a woman comes to Regeneron Pharmaceuticals Chief Diversity, Equity and Inclusion Officer Smita Pillai on the verge of taking a work hiatus, Smita tries to get at the root of—and the potential longevity of—the problem. Smita finds it usually can be boiled down to a certain incident—one straw that broke the camel's back. So she asks the woman to think of the incident using the "10, 10, 10, 10 Rule."

"Is this issue going to matter 10 hours later? 10 days later? 10 months later? 10 years later? Rarely will it still be a problem 10 months or 10 years later. So I encourage women to give themselves at least 10 days of brainstorming to find possible solutions. When things cool down, women realize the problem may not be as big as they initially thought."

If you love what you do, weather the ups and downs.

Kohl's Chief Financial Officer Jill Timm advocates for a realistic perspective as you evaluate your work and life: "There will be bad days when you feel like you haven't been an A-plus mom or an A-plus employee. That's life. But it all evens out, and you're usually harder on yourself than you need to be. Remember that on most days, pursuing your career passions makes you a more fulfilled person, and in turn a happier and better mother."

Make sure you know and use your company's work–life benefits.

Hewlett Packard Enterprise Chief Financial Officer Marie Myers had three kids in "Zoom school" during the pandemic, and her twins fell behind. Her son has dyslexia, and the learn-at-home environment was too difficult to navigate.

Marie first asked teachers to tutor her son twice a week. Then she learned through her company's parenting program that tutors are available to employee families at a discounted rate.

"As a result of the pandemic, employers really stepped up their employee resources—everything from wellness programs to caregiving resources for children and aging parents and the tutoring that I needed. When you're feeling the stress of work and life, be sure to check out the many ways your employer may be able to help."

Face your financial reality and ask for typical and atypical help.

When Suzanne Powers, the former Global Chief Product Officer of McCann Worldgroup (now running her own firm, Powers Creativity), divorced her first husband, a financial adviser asked, "Do you know how much money you need to live?" At the time she had 8-year-old twins and trying to come up with the amount she needed to live on was first terrifying, then empowering.

"You have to face the numbers and ask for help." As many would do, Suzanne asked her family for financial help, and she was fortunate that they were able to do so. But then she went a nontraditional route and asked her employer for financial help, too.

"I was in a senior position, and I told my boss that if I was going to continue to grow the business, I would need help with childcare expenses. I said it should be considered as part of my T&E and they agreed."

Find "half answers" for a work-life compromise.

Early in her career, when Gunjan Kedia was in a high-stress management consulting role, she traveled intensely—sometimes to four different cities in a week. She had a baby at home, and she finally reached a breaking point.

One of her clients was the CEO of a financial institution and he had once said, "Call me if you ever want to leave your firm." On a particularly stressful day, she called him from the sidewalk in New York City and joined his firm three months later. She was still in a senior position, but there was less travel.

"I didn't want to leave the workforce entirely, so I needed a half answer that would give me a compromise and an overall less hectic life."

The need for a work compromise is especially huge when someone in your family has a serious illness. The natural inclination is to put professional work on hold, but it's not always the best choice for your finances, career, or mental health. When Vonage Chief Marketing Officer and Head of Integration Joy Corso was faced with many family health issues, including a family member who had a terminal diagnosis while her mother had severe arthritis and her father was battling leukemia—leaving the workforce entirely for an undetermined amount of time was not a financial option. But the role she was in was extremely demanding and untenable. She made a difficult decision to leave her full-time job—working independently for 12 months on a variety of projects that leveraged her network. The consulting avoided an income gap, gave her more flexibility, and kept her skills and career relevant.

Half answers can also be found by saying no at your current company. When former Wells Fargo Chief Executive Officer of Consumer and Small Business Banking Mary Mack's daughters were young, she and her husband decided they would not move for her job. She kept getting offered bigger jobs in other locations, but she felt comfortable saying no because she was holding firm to a pact she and her husband made. Without any hesitation or resentment, she was able to say no even when she was giving up a big opportunity.

Mary says you have to know what is most important to you and own it. She often recalls the words of Stephen Covey: "It's easy to say no when there is a deeper yes burning within."

Explore a part-time schedule with your current employer.

Ryder System Chief Marketing Officer Karen Jones tries to erase the stigma around part-time work.

"It used to be that part-timers lost out on face time. But now we're in a different, often remote world where it's easier to have face time out of the office, and it's accepted that everyone is generally working more independently. Recognize that companies are willing to work with you about a reduced schedule and it's very possible you can stay at the same level. When women come to me saying they must leave the workforce, I try to give them a part-time option instead."

Realize an entrepreneurial venture can be more work than a corporate job.

Many women entertain the idea of an entrepreneurial venture—thinking that "being their own boss" will totally fix a life that seems off kilter.

Northwestern Mutual's Chief Strategy Officer Aditi Javeri Gokhale left the corporate world for about 18 months when her son was born. During that time, she collaborated with former colleagues to start a digital marketing firm that outsourced a lot of work to India. She had more daytime flexibility, but because of the time difference in India and the schedule of a newborn, she didn't have a lot of sleep.

"It was an exciting venture and a great foundation for my future work in digital marketing. But in many ways, it was much more work than the typical corporate job. As a new company with no track record, we had to work extra hard to establish our brand. There was no corporate structure, no assistant. The task of building and scaling start-ups requires a complexity of work that adds up to a monumental job."

Save valuable family time by shortening your commute.

Many employers adopted a post-pandemic hybrid work arrangement that combines work at home and work in the office. But any day that involves a commute is extra time away from your family.

Long before working at home was a global trend, Sharon Ryan's family decided to move from Chicago (where she had a one-hour commute each way) to Memphis (where she had a 10-minute commute each way). She was able to work for the same company in a different location.

"That shortened commute made way for huge family time." Her proximity to home and school also allowed her to go back and forth in the middle of the day if she needed to be close by for an emergency.

Consider leaving the workforce just one of many options.

UnitedHealth Group Chief Sustainability Officer Patricia L. Lewis has also seen many women on the brink of leaving the workforce. Though she will support any woman who feels this is the best decision for her life, she tries to get them to explore how a different work structure could lead to more flexibility.

"First define your short- and long-term goals and determine if you want less demanding work or a less rigid schedule. Maybe you don't want to work toward taking a very demanding higher position in six months. You could take a slower path that offers more flexibility, or you may want to move into a different area with more predictable hours. Whatever you decide, be able to articulate what you want and ask your boss for help in finding the best options."

The Weather Group's President of News and Original Series, Nora Zimmett, agrees it may be a certain job structure you need to change rather than giving up your entire career.

When she was a Field Producer for Fox News, Nora was on the road 142 days a year. This was a tough schedule for a new mother—but three weeks into her maternity leave she decided that being a stay-at-home mother could not be her entire identity.

Rather than returning to full-time work and heavy travel immediately, Nora started freelance writing for FoxNews.com. With the help of a part-time nanny and her husband's proximity in a home office, she was working a full-time—but flexible—freelance schedule.

After freelancing for a couple of years, Nora missed being part of a team and took a position at Bloomberg that required a lot less travel and gave her more time at home with her two-year-old.

Now Nora is in a position to help other women find the right work-life fit. If it's not possible to make a current job more flexible, she helps women explore other possible jobs in the company. This was the case when a very high-potential senior producer approached her about leaving. This woman's husband was traveling to the Middle East constantly, and she needed a more flexible job. Nora set it up so the woman could freelance—an arrangement that lasted over five years.

"This woman was not available all the time—especially for overnight or weekend assignments. But she was a frequent presence. Now she is back full time running a team—not missing a beat and not being penalized for her freelance years. Going freelance even for many years doesn't make you a second-class citizen, and it keeps you in the game. The technology in the television business, for example, changes every 60 to 90 days...so even a one-year hiatus can put you far behind."

During the pandemic several women on Nora's team also said they were struggling to blend work and life—and needed to opt out. Nora would always ask, "Is this what you really want, or is it because you think it's your only option?" More often than not, they could come up with an alternative work arrangement that worked on both sides.

Ultimately, as Anne Foulkes says, "It's your job, not your life. Your life is your family...and you can't be a good professional if you're not doing what you need to do for your family. Take care of what you need to take care of at home—just as long as you show me how the work will get done."

If you do take a hiatus, be strategic.

For some women, a hiatus from the workforce is clearly the best option for themselves and their families.

Martine Ferland struggled with the decision to take a hiatus from work after having her third child. At the time, she was a very well-regarded mid-level consultant, about 10 years into her career, and just starting to lead large clients. She felt very conflicted: she loved her job and loved being a mother. It was hard to ignore the vision in her head of what a good mom looks like: her mother did not work and was there when she got home with the traditional cookies and milk.

Ultimately, Martine decided to take time off—but only with the knowledge that she would be purposeful and precise about her timeline. At the outset she made a deal with herself, her family, and her colleagues: her hiatus would be for five years—ending when her youngest was in full-time school.

Martine did not regret her decision to take time off, but she missed work and wanted to be sure her skills and experience would not get too stale. For four years during her hiatus, she freelanced, working on the same type of consulting projects she left behind. She gradually increased her freelance commitment... 10 hours, then 15, then 30. At the five-year point, her mentor called and said it was time for her to come back to her full-time job—and she was ready.

When Martine returned to basically the same position she had left, one of her former colleagues, whom she had considered an equal in terms of talent and expertise, had become a partner while she was out. Martine reflected on the fact that she, too, would probably be a partner by that point had she not left.

It took only another three years for Martine to make partner as well. And then just five years after that she was leading a big office. Interestingly, the fact that she dialed down her career for five years may have delayed her journey to the next rung, but once she was back, she regained her momentum quickly. (And the man who made partner in her absence later worked for her.)

Though Martine was happy to get back to full-time work, she admits the transition wasn't always easy. Many years later she helped Mercer implement initiatives to keep women on hiatus in contact with colleagues and the business overall—and help them reacclimate once they return. They now have KIT Days—Keep-in-Touch Days—10 days each year when women on hiatus are paid to visit the office, sit in on meetings, and hear industry updates. They also have a buddy system where returners are assigned a colleague to help smooth their transition back to the office.

Karen Jones is also a proponent of keeping your hand in the work world. About one month into her own hiatus, she had the opportunity to help her former employer on a contract basis as they launched new products. This turned out to be a 20- to 30-hour-a-week gig for two years. The work was at about the same level as when she had been working full time.

Then she was offered a full-time job to come back at a higher level and salary. Her career actually blossomed because of her hiatus—by staying relevant, targeting her work to very important projects, and giving her a little room to breathe after a very intense professional period.

After Hewlett Packard Enterprise Chief Financial Officer Marie Myers lost a child, she also decided to take off a very specific amount of time (10 months). She discussed this timeline with her boss, and he promised her a job when she returned.

"I needed the time off after a big personal loss, but I knew it would not be good for my mental health or my career to make the hiatus open-ended. When I did return, I felt I had given myself the time to heal and I was ready to go back."

When you return to work after a hiatus, put your ego aside.

The Weather Group's President of News and Original Series Nora Zimmett notes that industries like television are particularly demanding, and some women simply need to take a break. A senior producer who was once on her team, for example, left television and pursued residential real estate for a while.

Then this woman wanted to get back into television and resume her career as the director of live programming. She soon realized her time out created a knowledge gap, and she would need to get up to speed on the new technology. Her best option was to return as a senior producer—not managing a team—and she swallowed the fact that she was working for someone who had once been her more junior associate producer.

Within a short six-month period of "repaying her dues," this woman rose again to the level of executive producer. "Women who can put their egos aside and not fixate on the title they once had will ramp back up quickly. As a rule, I don't hire or rehire brilliant jerks."

Consider smaller companies for an easier post-hiatus return.

In Kris Malkoski's experience, Segment Chief Executive Officer, Learning & Development at Newell Brands, a smaller company can be very welcoming as you work your way back from a hiatus.

At age seven, Kris's twins had health issues. She left the workforce for two years to fully focus on getting them well. At that point she had been at the level of VP and General Manager.

When Kris was ready to go back to work, her former employer did not have a job for her, and she found that other large employers saw her two-year hiatus as a stumbling block.

She then decided to diversify her search and consider nontraditional options. A friend in private equity had a company in his portfolio that wasn't doing well. He asked her to come in, kick the tires, and figure out how to turn the company around. She did that for a couple of years, got recent experience on her resume, and proved her skills had not gone stale. She realized a small company—without a lot of bureaucracy—gave her the chance to navigate her way back. Soon after, she got another big job offer running Craftsman for Sears.

Vonage Chief Marketing Officer and Head of Integration Joy Corso also knows flexibility can come in small packages. After she spent a year as an independent consultant (while family members were ill), she was ready to return to a full-time job. Her skills were the same (the consulting kept her current and marketable), but her attitude about work had changed. She liked the flexibility she enjoyed as a consultant and wasn't sure she would have the same freedom at a big corporation.

Joy decided to take a job at a much smaller company that was not a household name. Though companies of all sizes now offer flexibility, a company with fewer employees has less bureaucracy and more ability to set flexibility benefits across the board. "Working for a big-name company can be sexy, but a smaller employer can very easily offer flexibility when you most need it. And there's also the benefit of a broader job scope."

Chapter 7

Capitalize on New Work and Life Sensibilities

- Ride the wave of post-pandemic flexibility.
- Speak to your boss before you get to a breaking point.
- Build relationships with senior leaders who will support your case for flexibility.
- Let down your guard and be vulnerable with your colleagues.
- Consider your request for flexibility a sign of strength.
- Avoid simply dumping a problem into your boss's lap.
- Approach your boss with a business mindset.
- Ask for flexibility, even if there's no formal company policy.
- Be flexible about flexibility.
- Emphasize reciprocal flexibility.
- Change your work structure and create an opportunity for someone else.
- Recognize that men don't stress about flexibility; they just go for it.
- Know when you've earned the right for flexibility.

A S MENTIONED EARLIER, WOMEN FEAR asking for a flexible work schedule will put them out of the running for a promotion. This is not just the fear of a handful of women: the Deloitte Women@Work Survey[1] says the vast majority of women—95 percent—have experienced this trepidation, and 93 percent of women don't believe their day-to-day workloads will be adjusted if they ask for options such as a nontraditional work schedule or reduced hours.

All C-suite women I interviewed for this book told me this fear is not warranted. Don't be afraid to ask for what you need: women at the top are listening and helping women find solutions that accommodate 4 Jobs.

As a career coach, I advise women to research the kind of flexibility their companies have institutionalized and how their colleagues are generally making less formal arrangements work. The key to change is knowledge: know what can work at your company, what works at peer companies, and, specifically, what could work for you and your team.

When you approach your boss, be armed with all this information. As the women who contributed to this chapter emphasize, well-informed requests lead to the work that fits your life.

Ride the wave of post-pandemic flexibility.

Sharon Callahan-Miller—a former Chief Executive Officer of CDM New York (part of the global advertising firm Omnicom Health)—says the pandemic put women in the workplace flexibility driver's seat.

Currently an Executive Coach at her own firm, What's Possible, Inc., Sharon observes that The Great Resignation made it simply too hard to find—and keep—talented women. In my experience, a seasoned professional who knows what they're doing three days a week, for example, is preferable to training someone new who can work a full week. We're in an era when women can make their own rules and ask for what they need—without fear of being left behind.

Speak to your boss before you get to a breaking point.

Hormel Foods Chief Financial Officer Jacinth Smiley agrees that giving up on your aspirations may not be necessary if you instead give up on an inflexible situation. She says the only way out is an honest conversation with your boss.

Jacinth had a pregnant woman on her team who said she was feeling ill and exhausted and needed more work flexibility until her baby was born. "In a situation like this, you need to speak up and say what you need to be the most productive. Tell your boss you need to move your schedule around a bit to accommodate an afternoon nap, but also make assurances that the work will get done."

When McKinsey Chief Technology and Platform Officer Jacky Wright had to fly from Florida to Minnesota every week, a younger colleague also made the same trek. One day this mother started crying and said she just couldn't keep up the pace. The timing was wrong for all that travel with a baby at home.

"It was obvious she tried hard to hang on by a thread. Women shouldn't be afraid to speak up when something is not working—early in their discomfort. Chances are the discomfort will not suddenly disappear."

The current trend toward flexible work arrangements—such as remote work, compressed work weeks and job sharing—has created the opportunity for women to discuss more favorable options with their leaders.

For a productive conversation, Jacky advises women to approach their boss with a clear idea of the flexibility they need, the workload they want, what they would consider negotiable/nonnegotiable in the work arrangement, and whether a job share could possibly be a viable option. In many cases, she sees women finding a way to stay in a more senior-level job.

And if a woman approaches Jacky expressing a desire to step back from a big promotion, she's there to support that decision. She advises women to recognize and honor their current needs. "You have to understand what truly matters to you and make sure your priorities align. For me, that is health, then family, then work."

Build relationships with senior leaders who will support your case for flexibility.

When it comes to getting the work flexibility you need, it pays to have a strong internal network.

Mutual of Omaha's Chief Administrative Officer Liz Mazzotta believes mentors and sponsors can do more than advance your career… they can also help you achieve a positive work–life blend.

"When you ask your boss for flexibility, you want that request strengthened by support and recognition from a wide range of influential people within the organization who know your value and your work ethic. Always build your internal network: try to meet with two new people every month to build a community of supporters."

Let down your guard and be vulnerable with your colleagues.

Being honest with yourself, your boss, and your colleagues about work-life challenges you're facing opens the door to many different perspectives and solutions. If you share your trials and tribulations, others will likely share theirs.

Jill Timm is not afraid to share details of her hectic life, and she also tells her colleagues many stories about her less-than-perfect moments. She gets many laughs (and human connections) when she tells the story about the Christmas card she proudly created—despite the holiday bustle. Once the cards were all printed, she realized she mistakenly included a photo of her daughter's teammate, not her daughter.

Consider your request for flexibility a sign of strength.

Liz Mazzotta points out that asking for flexibility is not admitting defeat. In a few powerful words she says: "It's actually admitting reality. You can continue to learn and grow in your current position—as long as you have the confidence and conviction to say, 'Here's how I'm going to do it.'"

Avoid simply dumping a problem into your boss's lap.

As a mother of five children, Franklin Templeton Chief Executive Officer Jenny Johnson is very sympathetic to women who feel they need more flexibility in their work schedule. However, presenting a problem or challenge along with possible solutions is much more constructive.

"Your boss doesn't know the intricate details of your family life and what kind of arrangement would be best for you. Simply saying you need more flexibility puts the onus on your boss to figure it out and does not showcase your resourcefulness. Before you meet with your boss, think about how your job could be restructured or other job functions that may better fit your life. The key thing is to show there are many ways you can contribute in a meaningful way."

Approach your boss with a business mindset.

When you're feeling work and life are out of whack, Discover Financial Services Chief Diversity and Social Impact Officer Jonita Wilson says you should first talk to your inner circle—friends and family—about how to frame the issue. Get to the root of the problem, what you need to solve the problem, and what your ask should be.

It's important, too, to consider what your next course of action will be if you can't get the help you need. Decide which information you can hold back—the things your boss doesn't need to know. Ask yourself, "If I share this information, what's the benefit?"

It's probably enough to say you need to spend more time with your ailing mother, for example. There's no need to get into the nitty-gritty. Then ask for what you need. Zeroing in on the key problem gets your boss into immediate problem-solving mode. What company resources are there? What does your boss know about community resources—or what guidance can he or she offer from personal experience?

"All this advance planning, thinking, and strategizing gives you true business structure and a feeling of control. And you really want to approach your boss when you're feeling in control."

Ask for flexibility, even if there's no formal company policy.

Thirty years ago, when flexibility suggested only a propensity for gymnastics, Mary Mack worried she wouldn't be able to handle work and two children. Her second child had just been born, just 25 months after the first.

She didn't let the lack of any flexibility policy stop her from requesting a shorter workweek. Mary was a bit of a pioneer, telling her boss she wanted to work four days a week and giving him a plan for how it would work.

"I didn't just ask for flexibility, I took the guesswork out of it and made sure my boss knew how all the work would get done." Even at a time when workaholics were held in high esteem, she made it easy for her boss to agree. That reduced schedule helped her through a couple of years, and her career did not suffer (she retired from a Chief Executive Officer position).

Former Sysco Chief Supply Chain Officer Marie Robinson agrees that speaking up about your needs and managing expectations are key. Early in her career when she was working in logistics, she was the only woman in the room. And the only one leaving at 5:30 to get to the daycare pickup by 6:00. She never really discussed this with her boss and colleagues—they assumed she was a mother picking up her kids—but the unspoken need for her to leave at a certain time every day left her feeling guilty and unsettled.

Marie always encourages women on her team to be more open—with the understanding that while deadlines can't be missed, there is flexibility in how the work can get done. She realized she also had to manage expectations about her own work structure. She routinely got up at 4:30

each morning, had a cup of coffee, and then started answering emails. She quickly had to let her staff know they were not expected to respond before daylight.

Be flexible about flexibility.

Jessica Graziano encounters many women looking for the perfect work-life situation—but she notes that trade-offs are usually necessary to reach a point where things are not perfect, but workable.

Jessica hears: "I can't do a lateral move." "I can't do daycare." "I can't start earlier in the morning so I can leave the office earlier."

"I hear a lot of can'ts and not enough problem-solving and compromises."

Emphasize reciprocal flexibility.

At a time when there was very little flexibility at law firms in general, Dana Rosenfeld asked for and got a 75 percent schedule at a firm serving corporate clients.

She stuck to her reduced schedule most of the time, making it clear there was a give-and-take. When necessary, she would work more hours at home or on the weekends. Her employer knew she could be counted on to service clients properly, but they also knew they had to keep up their end of the bargain.

Change your work structure and create an opportunity for someone else.

As a single mother, Sharon Callahan-Miller felt the weight of providing for her family, and she wanted to do everything possible to keep her career moving. At one point this meant traveling to Europe every other week. She got on the plane without complaint, but after many years of an intense schedule she couldn't keep up the pace or be away from her sons for weeks at a time.

Sharon knew this was a pivotal moment—potentially being perceived as too weak to handle the job. But she let herself be vulnerable and resourceful at the same time. Instead of going to her boss with a resignation letter, she simply asked for backup to continue high performance in her job. This created an opportunity for a younger colleague to take on more global responsibilities—and kept Sharon closer to home.

"One of the things I've learned through the years is to always groom people who can step in your shoes when you need to give a little more to your family. You won't be punished for developing more leaders. (And, in fact, letting herself be honest about her work–life situation ultimately advanced her career... to a post as CEO of a US-based advertising agency, CDM New York.)

Recognize that men don't stress about flexibility; they just go for it.

In the post-pandemic era, employers are not at all surprised that women, especially, need a flexible work arrangement. Still, asking for one can seem like a monumental ask.

Former Stanley Black & Decker Chief Communications Officer Shannon Lapierre said she stressed herself out thinking about how she would be perceived in asking for a flexible schedule. She deliberated, stalled, and then finally asked. After all that agita, what was her boss's reply? A simple "Oh, okay."

Shannon also had an aha moment when two men on her team were co-coaching their sons' baseball team. They were working on a big project and one father said to the other, "You go and coach tonight and I'll stay." Shannon recalls, "No guilt, no hand-wringing—one father just left the office."

This gave her the push to leave the office when she could as well. Once, after her last meeting of the day, she realized if she left the office, she could make the last couple of innings of her daughter's softball game. She left and no one noticed or cared.

Regeneron Pharmaceuticals Chief Diversity, Equity and Inclusion Officer Smita Pillai has also noticed that men often have an easier time setting parameters and boundaries for their jobs—without any apologies. Women can be less bold, especially if they're afraid to ask for regular flexibility they can count on.

"When you ask for flexibility, don't start the discussion from a position of weakness. Don't apologize or appear to be asking for sympathy. Be firm: say this is what I need, and this is how the work will continue to get done."

Former US Board Chair of Deloitte Janet Foutty agrees that asking for flexibility takes some courage—and conviction. When she was just out of business school and newly married, she had a new job in Chicago. Her husband left a job in Indiana to move to Chicago, which was a big professional transition. Janet wanted to take the time to establish new roots and help her husband adjust to a new job and a new city.

She asked for her first assignments to be local so she wouldn't have to leave Chicago frequently. For about 18 months she was able to stay close to home, which gave the couple the time to get grounded. "I didn't ask for less challenging work, and, in fact, I worked many long hours. I simply wanted work that fit my life at that moment, and I wasn't afraid to ask for it."

Know when you've earned the right for flexibility.

Joy Corso adds that if you do a good job and work hard, you've earned the right for flexibility. "The key," she says, "is to never be outworked. Not in terms of the number of hours—but in terms of the quality of your work and your commitment. Flexibility will always be there if you don't drop the ball and your boss can always count on you."

It's not only about impressing your boss, though. Joy points out that it's also about cultivating great relationships—developing trust—with your colleagues so you can all enjoy collaboration and flexibility. "Trust among colleagues is incredibly powerful, so you can rely on each other. And if you manage people, do it in a way that fosters independence and individual capability. With these safeguards, your team will not fall apart if you go to soccer games on Tuesdays."

Chapter 8

Don't Be Afraid to Lean In-Between

- Walk or run at your own pace.
- Define success beyond title and money.
- Hold firm about your family needs—even if it slows your career temporarily.
- Consider foundational roles while your children are young.
- Find ways to keep growing if you opt for a less senior role.
- Pay less attention to flattery than a snug work–life fit.
- Sequence your career while you're in the workforce.
- Don't consider part-time lost time.
- Put off the corner office for a while or forever.
- Realize no work–life decision is carved in stone.
- Think forward if you step back.

IN A LEANIN.ORG AND MCKINSEY study, about 80 percent of women reported a desire to be promoted in the subsequent year. The data is more nuanced, however, suggesting the women looking for promotions are largely not in a caregiving phase of their lives. Not surprisingly, mothers with young children place an exceptionally high premium on flexibility. Without it, 62 percent of the moms said they would have to reduce their work hours or quit.[1]

Caregivers at the other end of the spectrum—those caring for aging parents—need the same level of job flexibility. Seventy percent of working caregivers suffer work-related difficulties due to their dual roles.[2]

Leaning into the next promotion sounds good in theory, but it's hard with 4 Jobs.

The ability to change the structure of a current job is often leaning, as I say, "in-between" or growing in place. It's hard to take on greater responsibility and do your job in less time. The women who do lean in-between are still ambitious (and as I write in my first book, *Ambition Redefined: Why the Corner Office Doesn't Work for Every Woman & What to Do Instead,*[3] there are many definitions of ambition and success).

Most women interviewed for this book did lean in to get to the C-suite—on their own timetable. It's refreshing to see that few followed a straight line to the top. They had stops and starts and times when they stayed in but stepped back in title. And not one suffered career penalties for putting their families first.

The message I heard loud and clear: *your career does not have to be a race.* You can reach your ultimate career goals in five years or 15. And there's no requirement to reach a certain title or salary. You can be a valued individual contributor or the head of a team. Your choice, your goals.

Walk or run at your own pace.

When Jonita Wilson's children were very young, she was at the manager and senior manager levels. For about five years she didn't seek out big new opportunities. She wanted to be available and present for her kids and never miss an athletic game.

But that didn't mean that Jonita's career was stagnant. Instead of worrying about her next big job title, she made sure she was always learning, shoring up the foundation for future opportunities, and maximizing her current job performance. She kept building her professional network within and outside the company. And she never deliberately told her leaders she was holding back in any way—she just personally monitored the pace of her career progression.

Later when bigger opportunities were presented to Jonita, she was ready, and didn't turn them down—all the way to her current Chief Diversity and Social Impact Officer post at Discover Financial Services. "Those were the times when I would have serious conversations with my husband explaining what bigger responsibilities would look like. I'd ask him to step up in certain ways. But it was on our timetable—when we approached it with our eyes wide open and had the family bandwidth to figure it out."

Define success beyond title and money.

In business, success is most often measured in financial terms. But Gregg Renfrew sees it differently.

"I've redefined success as doing something that is meaningful to me and to the world. You need to make money, and it's important for your business to be financially successful, but you can also make a lasting social impact and enjoy what you're doing. At Beautycounter we always viewed success through a triple bottom line that benefits people, the planet, and profit for the business."

McKinsey Chief Technology and Platform Officer Jacky Wright also links success to a very personal life vision. "Not everyone has to be in the C-suite. Harness the power of being true to your values and making room for what's most important to you."

Hold firm about your family needs—even if it slows your career temporarily.

In former Chief Executive Officer of CBRE's Global Workplace Solutions business Chandra Dhandapani's view, there's no harm in stepping back or slowing down.

Lots of women agree in theory but are afraid to say this to a manager. It seems easier to do whatever is asked, even if it infringes on family time. Chandra, on the other hand, always stood her ground when it came to her family needs.

Once, when she was leaving the office at 5:30 because she needed to be home to nurse her baby, her manager asked where she was going and why. He didn't like her answer and said she had to be present for a team meeting at 6:30. She firmly said she needed to leave and offered to call in later.

Another time, Chandra was home with her sick infant on a Saturday morning and her manager insisted she had to come to the office to handle a problem. She again firmly told her manager it wasn't possible, but she would get one of her direct reports to go in.

Clearly her manager did not like that she was not making herself available under any circumstances 24/7, and he suggested she step back from a P&L management role into a more flexible operations position. They didn't want to lose her, so they offered her six job options. She agreed to the change in role and chose to head up operations for about 15 months.

Before too long she was offered a Chief Information Officer role, which came at the right time because her son was a little older. Chandra was pleased that the short detour to a new area had not ruined her advancement chances and gave her the benefit of learning a new job function. Through the years, she has also helped women on her team step back for a bit with modified part-time roles, gradually coming back to full-time positions as their family situations ease.

"Women need to realize that these decisions to scale back can be temporary arrangements with no career penalties."

Consider foundational roles while your children are young.

"Recognize that with good health our lives are long, and it's okay to stop pushing for the higher and higher position at different life junctures."

That's sound advice from former Sysco Chief Supply Chain Officer Marie Robinson, who focused on a variety of experiences rather than job titles while she had young children. When she and her second husband were first married, they moved to California, which meant leaving a company where she had worked most of her career. She took this as an opportunity to look for a smaller company and a less complex role—a move that was technically a step back. In retrospect she learned a tremendous amount from this experience.

Later, when her oldest son was in seventh grade and it was clear he would be a challenging adolescent, she decided to take another pause. Again, she went to a smaller company where her job was technically more junior but turned out to be broader in scope.

"Realize you'll reach a point in your career when your children have much more independence. Then you'll look ahead to a long unobstructed runway and capitalize on all your foundational experience."

Find ways to keep growing if you opt for a less senior role.

Christine Hurtsellers also scaled back her career when she had three young children. At the time she had a demanding job at an investment firm and a long commute. She left so early and got home so late that she didn't see her kids from Sunday to Friday night—a situation that furthered her career but was untenable at home.

Christine then decided to make a career change to a less demanding position close to home. "To some it may have looked like a stupid career move, but I intentionally wanted to learn a new skill set, pull back a bit, and keep my toe in the game."

Rather than opting out completely, Christine spent six years in a more junior portfolio management role and was home every night for dinner. When her kids were a bit older and she was ready, she returned to investment management and was not penalized for her time away. Looking back, the former Voya Investment Management Chief Executive Officer sees her step back as a time of growth and learning, when she gained valuable building-block knowledge that later helped to advance her career.

"Don't be hard on yourself. You're not a failure if it takes a little longer for you to reach your career goals while you're raising your family."

Pay less attention to flattery than a snug work–life fit.

When The J.M. Smucker Co. Chief People and Company Services Officer Jill Penrose still had young children, she consciously opted for a strategy role, rather than a big travel job that would frequently take her away from home.

She had been offered a General Manager role requiring travel to various plants, and she discussed career path alternatives with her manager. "Part of me wanted to take that big job, thinking I could figure out a way to make it work. But then I did my research to see what kind of commitment was behind the title, and I knew not to let myself be flattered into a role that did not fit my life."

Sequence your career while you're in the workforce.

Women frequently think of career sequencing as periods in and out of the workforce—with long absences that can adversely affect career traction and long-term financial security. But women can also stay in the workforce and practice sequencing—taking different jobs for shorter periods in different phases of life.

When Kelley Drye & Warren Firm Managing Partner Dana Rosenfeld's family was young, she actively chose employers and jobs affording more flexibility. She started out at a medium-size litigation firm, but then left when the demands of the job got more complex, requiring overnight travel. She then switched to policy work in a more contained government law position.

"Corporate law may have been more prestigious in the eyes of my law school classmates, but it didn't mesh with my young family. Everything I did in less stressful roles still built the cornerstone for my career. You can build a solid portfolio of skills in any job."

Don't consider part-time lost time.

When her first child was born, Jill Penrose was at the Director level, and she decided to go part-time for a year when she first returned from maternity leave. She didn't want to leave the workforce entirely, and she was comfortable acknowledging it was a time in her life when she did not want to be the leader in a big job.

Three years later Jill was promoted to Vice President, a clear indication that her brief part-time status did not prevent her from growing in her career.

Now J.M. Smucker's Chief People and Administrative Officer says: "We often tell ourselves a story that if we do X, then Y will happen or never happen. But there's lots of time—our lives and careers unfold over decades. It's okay to give yourself a period when you hold back a bit. This is when we can really invest in learning and preparing for the next opportunity."

Put off the corner office for a while or forever.

Early in her career, when Dana Rosenfeld asked for a reduced work schedule at a prominent law firm, she was definitely not on the partner track. In fact, she did not get on that partnership track until her sons were in high school, becoming a partner at age 50.

Dana always felt there was time for her to reach her highest career goals, and she enjoyed the greater flexibility while her sons were young—taking them to doctor appointments, attending their sports games, and being a room parent in the elementary school years.

With an eye to the future, Dana actively found ways to continually develop her portfolio of skills and experience. "I knew I would eventually reach my career goals, and a specific timetable was less important than spending the extra time with my children."

Realize no work–life decision is carved in stone.

Women who want to be good mothers and good professionals often feel every work–life decision is an earth-shattering proposition.

Former Stanley Black & Decker Chief Communications Officer Shannon Lapierre says that when you don't put enormous weight on every decision, you give yourself more leeway to jump in and simply try out a situation.

"You'll have the freedom to change and adjust as you try things out. You might initially think daycare is the best choice for your work schedule, but then if you take on more responsibilities you might need greater coverage from a live-in nanny. When you're open to many possibilities, you give yourself the freedom to make choices that seem right for the circumstances in that moment. The best solution for today might not be a long-term solution."

Think forward if you step back.

If you decide you need to dial down the intensity of your career for a period, Linda Rutherford advises that you emphasize your continued commitment by talking about how you will keep adding to your portfolio of skills.

"Show you're not just thinking about what you need today—make it clear you've given personal goals for your entire career some good thought. Acknowledge your plans are fluid—you might not always have the same goals you have right now."

And if you do know now that you'll never want the top job, Linda says you can still strive to be a leader. "Don't be beholden to an up-or-out mentality. Think about leading a program or initiative without being on the manager track. Many individual contributor roles are invaluable to employers—and many ambitious women do not have big management positions."

Chapter 9

Make Organization Your Middle Name

- Document all family and household information in one place.
- Run household routines like clockwork to make more family time.
- Pick and choose where it's best to invest your time.
- Build partnerships with your children's teachers.
- Get help with the prep for school projects.
- Save mileage . . . and your sanity.
- Plan ahead on your shared office calendar.
- Get out from under the email avalanche.
- Decide what really needs to be a meeting.

HOW DO WOMEN MANAGE 4 Jobs, especially when one job is managing multimillion-dollar budgets and thousands of people?

If your answer is "with hot and cold running help," you're succumbing to persistent stereotypes. Yes, there are executive women who have a full household staff, multiple nannies, and tutors for each child. But among senior executive women throughout corporate America, that seems to be more the exception than the rule.

I found it fascinating that all C-suite women I interviewed for this book lead pretty humble lives at home. They cook meals and sit down to family dinners, they do laundry, they have intermittent cleaning help, and there are no butlers in sight. About one-quarter of these women have husbands or partners who either left the workforce entirely to take the lead on caring for family and households or switched careers to have more flexibility to help. But even in these cases, the women I spoke with have various responsibilities for family and households, too.

As revealed in this chapter, the secret sauce is summed up in one word: *organization*. These women brought their business skills home and created systems to keep everything on track for busy families and make households run without a hitch. None of their tips are rocket science: it's the simplicity that makes it all work.

Document all family and household information in one place.

When her children were young, Kris Malkoski, Segment Chief Executive Officer of Learning & Development at Newell Brands, had a 12-page factbook listing doctors, medications, emergency phone numbers, food allergies, names of mothers who were willing to help if she couldn't get home right away, where to buy household necessities, important contacts at school, and more.

On Sunday nights she would make a master schedule for the week to benefit all family members and caregivers. She noted when Dad or Mom would be away and travel and hotel information. All the kids' activities were listed with drop-off/pickup details. Events at school were highlighted with notes on what was required. And there was a heads-up about the service people who were coming to the house and what they needed to be told.

On the weekends, Kris would also cook for the week and portion food in plastic containers. The master schedule included nights she had a business dinner and cooking instructions for the meals.

"I organized more and, consequently, had less worry and stress."

Run household routines like clockwork
to make more family time.

PPG General Counsel Anne Foulkes realizes we have a finite amount of time—usually about 18 years—when our children are home full time. She has always put the major focus on her children for that time period—alongside her career. She believes it takes tremendous organization to feel like you've dotted all the i's and crossed all the t's, gaining some semblance of control over day-to-day life.

Like Kris Malkoski, every Sunday evening Anne would take a couple of hours to write out the schedules for both daughters each week. This up-front work reduced last-minute stress and allowed her to schedule the time she needed/wanted to be at their swim meets and tennis matches. Despite a busy professional schedule, her organization made room for her to attend most of their sports events—and have a role in swim meets (as a timer) so her daughter could see her active participation.

Pick and choose where it's best to invest your time.

Throughout the year, Aon's Global Chief Operating Officer Mindy Simon buys birthday cakes and treats to send to school. But at Christmas time, when she really wants to create traditions her children will remember, they make a wide array of cookies from scratch, and she takes the time to teach her kids to cook.

Mindy and her daughters also do a big cooking project on the weekends, delivering meals to elderly neighbors. Time spent on these projects helps them view the world outside of their family unit.

"It makes sense to invest time in valuable family traditions and give to others with gratitude."

Build partnerships with your children's teachers.

Gregg Renfrew says it's never a good idea to try to micromanage your children's teachers.

"Let educators educate and instead find ways to partner. Give them the space to create a relationship with your children and allow them to do what they do best. When you focus on a partnership you build trust and strengthen the relationship they have with both you and your children."

To build a constructive partnership, Gregg has always been transparent with her children's teachers, letting them know she works full time and travels often.

"I keep an open line of communication that keeps me organized about what is going on at school and what I need to talk through with my kids."

Get help with the prep for school projects.

Every mother knows school projects shoot family stress to the moon when planning is left until the eleventh hour. And busy working mothers, especially, know it's hard to gather all the materials for a science project or diorama after stores have closed.

One great idea is to take the initiative to ask teachers what big projects are coming up, so there are no last-minute surprises. Gregg Renfrew then would talk through projects with her kids and ask a caregiver or friend to pick up all the necessary materials well in advance.

"It's not the administrative piece of a project that's important—you want to spend the time actually doing the activity with your child in a non-stressful, non-rushed way."

Save mileage ... and your sanity.

Northwestern Mutual Chief Strategy Officer Aditi Javeri Gokhale doesn't drive from store to store to buy everything her family needs. She has a totally digital household and orders everything online—clothes, food, and household supplies.

"When you rely on brick-and-mortar stores, you waste a lot of time driving through traffic, finding parking spaces, choosing from often limited selections, and waiting in long lines. Time is finite. Given a choice, I'd rather spend it with family or friends than shopping in person for the basics."

Plan ahead on your shared office calendar.

Sharon Ryan was always understanding about the time her team needed to be with their kids—unless they snuck around and simply disappeared.

"Just manage expectations and put the fact that you have to leave at 4:00 p.m. on Tuesdays and Thursdays to help out with the school play on your shared calendar."

Get out from under the email avalanche.

Ryder System Chief Marketing Officer Karen Jones realized that in her hundreds of emails, quite a few were not sent to her specifically. She was copied on many emails she believed could not be as important.

"Now any email that has a 'cc' goes directly into a separate, less urgent folder I can read when I have more time."

Decide what really needs to be a meeting.

The pandemic changed a lot of things in the business world, but "Zoom fatigue" was the proof it did not eliminate unnecessary meetings.

Ocean Spray Chief Commercial Officer Monisha Dabek believes anyone at any level can speak up and suggest involving fewer people in a meeting—or question if a meeting is needed at all.

"Peers often clog your calendar with meetings—even more than managers. Sometimes a 10-minute conversation between two people can save five other people a precious hour."

Chapter 10

Get Off Your Island and Ask For Help

- Be a woman who asks.
- Make yourself helpable.
- Drop "I'm fine" from your lexicon.
- Get out of your own head and gather work–life wisdom.
- Hold on in the workforce with help from family and friends.
- Borrow ideas from many smart people.
- Venture out of your community silo.
- Create informal business networks that emphasize life.
- Gravitate toward sponsors rather than mentors.
- Do the colleague give-and-take.
- Bring men into the work–life brainstorming.

WHERE'S THE MEDAL FOR THE woman who does absolutely every-thing on her own? What kind of award do you get for keeping silent when you really need help?

There's no rest for the weary and no awards for the martyr. The result of cutting yourself off from a more collaborative approach to work and life is stress and burnout. We all need help from family, friends, acquaintances, colleagues, teachers, and others who are willing to help *when asked*.

There are many global political and economic quotes attributed to Hillary Clinton, but the one more everyday quote I refer to time and again is "It takes a village." Indeed, it takes a village to manage 4 Jobs and blend all aspects of work and life.

The advice in this chapter sheds light on the fellowship of women willing to help you. You could tap into this goodwill via senior women on your team or in discussions sponsored by employee resource groups. There are women willing to help you in your neighborhood, at your children's schools, and throughout your community.

You're not alone trying to get through your massive to-do list. Reach out, be a little vulnerable, and get the help you need.

Be a woman who asks.

There is a book that Nationwide Chief Customer Officer Amy Shore often recommends: *Women Don't Ask*.[1] She feels this book relates to all aspects of work and life.

"We need to ask our families to be a team. Ask our partners to be real partners. Ask our mentors for advice. Ask our colleagues to be supportive. In all areas of life, get off your island and ask for help."

Make yourself helpable.

Before you ask for help, you need to be sure you are actually ready and able to accept that help.

This is something that former Chief Executive Officer of CBRE's Global Workplace Solutions business, Chandra Dhandapani, learned when she heard Paralympic skier Bonnie St. John speak at a company event. The message is "Don't be a martyr...make it easier for others to help you." Show that you invite and need help—and that you in turn will help others, too.

"You're not weak if you're unable to handle absolutely everything life throws at you—it's actually a sign of strength and wisdom when you know your limits and you give people permission to help."

Drop "I'm fine" from your lexicon.

One of the 4 Jobs—dealing with eldercare issues—can often snowball. Linda Rutherford's mother and mother-in-law both had severe illnesses at the same time—requiring lots of attention and adding to her work and life stress. She brought her 75-year-old mother to the ER seven times.

"I learned to stop saying I was fine. When I was honest and let people know what I was dealing with, I got a lot of understanding and compassion. My colleagues realized I truly needed more flexibility, and people in all corners of my life stepped up and offered help."

Get out of your own head and gather work–life wisdom.

Many women rely on conversations about blending work and life in impromptu settings like the school bus stop, an exercise class, or an elevator ride at the office.

Mutual of Omaha Chief Administrative Officer Liz Mazzotta says, "You can also be intentional and get a group of women together on a regular basis to share ideas."

Liz was part of a group called Moms of Mid-Years (MOMY)—slightly older moms who had young children along with professional careers. They brought their children along and took turns hosting a Saturday morning meeting once a month to share stories and tips—and got each other through many work–life challenges.

Hold on in the workforce with help from family and friends.

Because the business world changes so quickly, Gregg Renfrew knows it can be difficult to reenter the workforce after even a few years at home. She often advises women on her team to ask for help from family and friends before making the decision to take a professional hiatus.

"The job you left even two years ago won't be the same as you left it. I encourage women to stay in the game in some capacity—scale back to part-time, become a freelancer, or take a consulting job. As working women, we need to know when to ask for help so leaving the workforce doesn't seem like a necessity. There are usually family members or friends who can support you, so I would not underestimate how their help could change a stressful situation. It's important to stay in the game intellectually and financially."

Borrow ideas from many smart people.

Successful professionals can have a wide range of good values, family cultures, and beliefs about success and money. So many factors shape a person, making it tricky to fully embrace a particular role model. Janet Foutty suggests building a mosaic instead—borrowing ideas from many smart professionals on how to advance your career in ways that do not overwhelm your life.

Sharon Ryan says you also can be a role model to others if you don't try so hard to make your life seem flawless. She has always let people see challenges she has faced so no one thought she led a picture-perfect life. "When we all let down the facades, we share real experiences and solutions."

Venture out of your community silo.

In many communities, there are two siloed groups of women—those who work professionally and those who don't. Kelley Drye & Warren Firm Managing Partner Dana Rosenfeld believes all moms can help each other, and for that reason she has cultivated a diverse group of friends.

Along with the normal carpooling, she had friends who would take her son for a day if he was sick, or it was a snow day and he couldn't be at school. She would help more on weekends—doing more of the travel baseball driving, for example.

"All mothers are busy, and all mothers need help. We can join forces during the hectic child-raising years."

Gregg Renfrew adds that parents of your children's friends don't have to be your soulmates, but it helps to have a little more than a cordial relationship. "All these parents are additional sets of eyes and ears for working mothers—and they can help you stay on top of everything going on at school and during extracurricular activities."

To build relationships, Gregg has always encouraged families of her children's friends to spend time at their home. "This gives me the opportunity to get to know their friends and their parents and makes me feel more connected. These are the friendships I've prioritized over the years."

Create informal business networks that emphasize life.

Franklin Templeton Chief Executive Officer Jenny Johnson has created informal social groups with women in the same business. There's no formal agenda—the objective is networking and building trust.

"I'm part of a group of women in asset management who have a retreat once a year. Periodically we have cocktails via Zoom. Activities run the gamut—even covering horseback riding, hiking, and fishing. There are some business conversations, but these topics don't dominate. It's a bunch of friends who talk about their work challenges—but mainly how to nurture both families and careers."

Through these informal gatherings the women create natural networks without overtly networking. It turns out that through this group they've helped each other professionally—they've filled several board seats and helped women transition to new jobs—all while sharing their wisdom on blending work and life.

Gravitate toward sponsors rather than mentors.

Many people can help you advance your career, but Jessica Graziano believes a higher-level sponsor can more powerfully advocate for you as you find ways to blend work and life.

"A mentor provides feedback and support but might not have the clout to go to bat for you if you need more flexibility in a job or decide to take a step back for a while. Sponsors can help you avoid any misperception that you're less dedicated to your career."

Do the colleague give-and-take.

Shannon Lapierre has seen lots of women suffer in silence about work–life conflicts, and she says your manager and your colleagues can't help you if you don't proactively say what's going on and create a reciprocal "helping" relationship.

Once a woman on her team mentioned late in the day that she was missing an important sports game for her son. Shannon told her to go, and the woman said, "How can I leave when we've got this big project?" Shannon said, "I'll cover for you, and you can cover for me another time."

Bring men into the work–life brainstorming.

Women tend to meet in groups of women to discuss work–life issues. But Jenny Johnson encourages men to talk openly about how they pitch in with their families and households—like picking children up from school or taking care of laundry.

"Male leaders need to model this 'accepted behavior' for other men."

Chapter 11

Outsource What You Can—
and Can't—Afford

- Invest in your career, even when you have limited funds.
- Allocate and reallocate the money that saves your sanity.
- Look for things you can outsource at little or no cost.
- Outsource intermittently.
- Give up less important tasks.
- Reward yourself with time when you get a raise.

WHEN YOU IMAGINE HOW MUCH women earn at the top of the corporate ladder, you probably think, "Well, of course they can afford to hire people to help them care for their homes."

And they do. A *Fortune* study found that two-thirds of US working women who have at least one direct report outsource various household tasks, including housecleaning, pet sitting, grocery delivery, and landscaping.[1]

The very important reality, though, is that the C-suite women I interviewed for this book told me they have *always* outsourced household tasks—even when their titles were much more junior. This is also reflected in the study: two-thirds of women at the manager level

outsource for some type of hired help—from childcare to cleaning services to personal trainers to grocery delivery services.

The consensus is that from the start of your career you need time for
two critical things: caring for your family and building your portfolio of
expertise. In any given week it's a tall order to do both—and as evidenced
in this chapter, it makes sense to allocate your time carefully and preserve your sanity through even limited outsourcing.

Women I interviewed told me they did not want to spend precious
family time, for example, cleaning the house every weekend. So they've
always been willing to cut back in other household budget areas to hire
a housecleaner every week or twice a month. They generally feel any
money used to outsource household tasks is a valuable investment in the
time better spent nurturing careers and families.

Invest in your career, even when you have limited funds.

Kris Malkoski and her husband have always been a two-career couple—
with big careers at that. Her husband was a CEO twice and traveled
nonstop.

Add in the fact that Kris had three children in less than two
years—all under age five when she was a Director of Marketing launching a major healthcare brand. At the time, her husband was commuting
to Asia—three weeks away, then two weeks back.

So how did Kris keep all the balls in the air? She paid for a lot of
help. In a mid-level position, though, she did not have a big executive
salary. She ignored the prevailing wisdom that it's not "worth it" to work
if childcare is eating up most of your salary or you're just breaking even.
Instead, Kris saw her high cost of outsourcing as an investment that
allowed growth in her career. And she knew her kids would not always
need the same amount of care.

Marie Myers had the same approach—investing 30 to 40 percent of her
paycheck in her early career years to pay for live-in nannies, who became

the family's house manager. "Invest in the foundation that will help you reach your peak earning years—when you're in your 50s and 60s."

Kris also had a live-in nanny—and because that nanny was caring for three very young children, she also hired another woman to come in for three hours a day to do laundry and cook dinner.

Later, Kris tapped into the teaching assistants who were always looking for extra ways to make money. She would enlist these young women to drive her children home from school and supervise homework.

"I always had a big outlay for the resources I hired, but it saved my sanity, gave our household structure and routine, kept our kids safe and happy, and gave me the room to keep growing in my career. If I hadn't invested the money then, I might not be where I am today."

Allocate and reallocate the money that saves your sanity.

Jonita Wilson learned very early on to put everything in perspective when it comes to running a household. She decided she didn't need to immediately take care of the dishes in the sink or the clothes in the laundry basket. As long as the house was decent-ish and everyone was healthy, she felt life was okay.

But then one day when things really were in disarray, Jonita exploded, and she and her husband decided it was time to get help. They've had a woman help with cleaning every other week since then. Initially they couldn't really afford the extra expense, but she says it was a wise investment that saved her sanity, her marriage, and, she says jokingly, the lives of her children.

"Even if outsourcing takes a big chunk out of your after-tax income, earmark that chunk early on, and keep reallocating it. When we no longer needed childcare, we put the same chunk of money into more household help. We have different needs and priorities at various times, but some form of help always has big paybacks in sound mental health."

Sharon Ryan agrees women should hire as much childcare and household help they can reasonably afford. "Your weekends should not be about cleaning the house. And for sanity and personal growth, a spouse or partner who stays home should have time to pursue interests and activities not house or family related."

The time women don't spend on housecleaning can be spent with their children, their partners—and in the community. In Sharon's case, she invested the time she saved on domestic tasks into volunteering at organizations benefiting women and children.

Look for things you can outsource at little or no cost.

When women hear the word *outsource*, they see big dollar signs. Despite the mental health benefits, not everyone feels comfortable spending money on household services.

Ocean Spray Chief Commercial Officer Monisha Dabek reminds women that not all outsourcing has a big price tag. "Your dry cleaner may pick up and deliver at no cost. You can buy carrots prechopped for a few more cents. I think of every possible way to save time."

Outsource intermittently.

Paying people to help you run your household *every* week can be expensive. But Amy Shore, Chief Customer Officer at Nationwide, says even intermittent help makes sense.

"A housecleaner once a month can still be freeing. Make a list of the things absolutely only you can do, and the things someone else could do well. You might find several things inexpensive to outsource, even part of the time."

Give up less important tasks.

Not everyone wants to hand over all childcare and household responsibilities to others. When she was a single mother, Corning's Chief Human

Resources Officer Jordana Kammerud's work and life juggle was hectic, but she still enjoyed making dinner for her daughter without anyone else hovering nearby.

The answer was to hire a woman to do the grocery shopping and make dinner two nights a week. Jordana found it the best of both worlds: she got a bit of a break and had the alone time she wanted with her daughter.

Dana Rosenfeld hired out tasks selectively as well. She found, for example, hiring a college counselor a smart move—giving herself distance from what can be extremely stressful essay writing. "Instead, we did the college visits together, which were great family time."

Reward yourself with time when you get a raise.

Shannon Lapierre always advised women on her team to put a chunk of their raise into a retirement fund.

That's the solid financial advice. Then she moved to the solid time management advice.

"Once you have more income, invest some of the money in outsourcing—a housecleaner, someone to cut the lawn or do the gardening, so that you free up more time to spend with your family. Time is the best gift you can give yourself."

Chapter 12

Insource to Your Family

- Don't assume every household problem needs to be solved by Mom.
- Give your kids the agency to learn household life skills.
- Rely on your family to reduce outside help.
- Cultivate a family team.

ANOTHER MISPERCEPTION ABOUT HIGHER-INCOME HOUSEHOLDS is that children are catered to without being given any family responsibilities. Though all children are busy with school, sports, and many other extracurricular activities, the C-suite women who spoke about running their households for this book have taken a divide-and-conquer, family team approach. No one advocates for the equivalent of child labor—just a nod toward pitching in.

The children in these families have grown up with age-appropriate responsibilities, and it's clear that instilling the value of contributing created strong work ethics. Julie Lythcott-Haims says it well in her book, *How to Raise An Adult*: "[children] must contribute, know how to contribute and feel the rewards of contributing in order to have the right approach to hard work when they head out into the workplace and become citizens of the community. Chores build the kind of work ethic that is highly sought after in our communities and in the workplace."[1]

When you read the contributor biographies section on page xxi, you'll see that chores led many children to build strong work ethics and follow the lead of their career-minded mothers.

Don't assume every household problem needs to be solved by Mom.

Not all two-income households are created equally. In fact, in the book *Fair Play*,[2] author Rodsky says women are the default parents (she actually coins the term "she-fault parents") expected to answer the call of duty whenever anything in the household or the family goes awry.

In the years when Joy Corso and her husband (owner of an IT consultancy) were both very busy working, traveling, and commuting, they each needed to step up at different times.

"We both may have thought whatever we were working on was the most important. If the situation was not an emergency (requiring us both to leave work), we talked about who really needed to be home. It was absolutely not an immediate assumption that I, as the mother, would do so."

Give your kids the agency to learn household life skills.

Many hands make light work.

That's has been a motto in Corning Chief Human Resources Officer Jordana Kammerud's household, where her children were taught from an early age to pitch in.

Though many parents feel chores are just about teaching responsibility, Jordana believes setting the table or cleaning the bathroom are life skills that will be needed whenever her children live with other people.

And sometimes your kids are surprisingly good at a particular chore: "Who would have thought my son would be a super laundry master?!"

Rely on your family to reduce outside help.

When Mary Jones, former Deere & Company General Counsel, had nannies taking care of her children, she didn't ask them to do housework. She brought in occasional housecleaners but otherwise did not have special help.

Now, with older children, Mary still doesn't have household help. Part of the reason is that she has made peace with a house that's a little messier. She's all too aware that her children won't live full time at home too much longer, so she would rather spend more time with them than vacuum her rugs.

But that doesn't mean she has a household free-for-all. Her children have grown up knowing they're expected to pitch in. Through the years, Mary's kids have, for example, picked up their toys, set the table, or stopped on the way home to pick up groceries for dinner. All family members do their own laundry, and Mary regularly cooks with two of her children.

"Our family relies on each other instead of a lot of outside help."

Cultivate a family team.

When Nationwide Chief Customer Officer Amy Shore's kids were growing up, they always knew they were part of a team. There was no question they were expected to contribute, and they had specific roles to play on the team (that became more complex as they aged).

"The kids knew my role was primarily working so we could have a house, cars, trips. It was their role to help make the household run—even in small ways."

As Amy's children grew up and did, for example, the occasional grocery shopping, the family did not need to pay for as much outside help. And the team approach has carried on through the years—as a family they've helped her daughter tear down buildings on her horse-boarding farm and do finishing work on renovations.

The message was never "you have to do your chores"—it was "we all help the team." And occasionally the Bonus Fairy would come and give monetary rewards.

Chapter 13

Get on the Anti-Perfection Train

- Live, love, laugh, and let go.
- Stop striving to be a perfect mother.
- Keep your eye on the real prize.
- Eliminate the word *should*.
- Cultivate happiness.
- Follow the adage "one day at a time."
- Give yourself the gift of focus.
- Ask for a gradual return after maternity leave.
- Hit your motherhood stride over time.
- Try not to overcompensate for being a working mother.
- Don't overestimate how much time your young children need with you.
- Know you can't do everything, but you can do what matters most.
- Don't give in to guilt.
- Play to the seasons in your life.
- Don't buy into the idea that more work hours lead to more success.
- Break free from traditional work norms.
- Blend work and life with can-do confidence.
- Have it all in a month, not a day.

- Live by the tenet that quality wins over quantity.
- Cut yourself some slack about missing school or sports events.
- Take pride in all the things you do.

JUST DON'T BEAT YOURSELF UP.

When you read the tips in this chapter you'll see that C-suite women have perfected the art of anti-perfection. In some cases, it took time to let go of impossibly high standards at work and at home, but all women eventually came to the realization that indeed "something's gotta give."

In the thick of my busiest years—when my husband and I were raising children, renovating our home, and building our careers—I used to make mile-long lists of what I felt needed to be accomplished over the weekend. Inevitably, the list was too long, I got too little done, and I felt like a failure by Sunday night. Soon, I reduced my expectations and chose one or two things that could reasonably be accomplished.

My career-coaching clients often tell me they must leave the workforce because they're not getting enough done at home. *Enough* is the operative word. Too often these women aren't getting things done with what they feel is 100 percent success. I remind them that if their children are safe and cared for, they can consider operating at 90, 80, or even 70 percent household efficiency.

As long as your home is not in complete chaos, it doesn't matter if the laundry stays in the basket overnight. The occasional pizza delivery won't stunt your children's growth. Sending store-bought treats to school is not a capital offense.

The message from women in this chapter is "pick and choose." Know where you *must* spend your time and know where you *want* to spend your time. Figure out where you can safely cut corners. And analyze what's really behind your quest for perfection.

Brené Brown has famously said, "Perfectionism is not the same thing as striving to be your best...it is not about healthy achievement and growth...it's a twenty-ton shield that we lug around thinking it will protect us."[1]

Far healthier is to follow the wisdom of time management guru Laura Vanderkam, who says, "Done is better than perfect."[2]

Most of all, stop listening to your most formidable critic...*yourself.*

Live, laugh, love, and let go.

Early in her career, Kris Malkoski received the *Working Mother* magazine "Mothering That Works" award. She talked about her motto, "Live, Laugh, Love, and Let Go" in both work and life. In a nutshell: don't dwell on things that really don't matter.

Kris once forgot it was the day for all mothers to bring homemade cookies to preschool. Instead, on the way to school, she stopped at the grocery store and bought Ding Dongs and Ho Hos. When she arrived with her store-bought packages, she got some surprised looks from other mothers. She decided to "let go" and ignore the judgmental eyes.

Important to note: the Ding Dongs and Ho Hos were the first to go.

Stop striving to be a perfect mother.

There's no perfect human. BorgWarner's Chief Administrative Officer Tonit Calaway says we're all bound to make mistakes—and both you and your children can find humor in the situation.

Because Tonit's workdays were so busy, she sometimes had calendar mishaps. She once drove her kids to school only to see that their car was the only one in the parking lot. She (and her kids) forgot school was closed that day.

Embarrassed and feeling like a bad mother, she apologized profusely to her children. It actually happened three times after that, and each time they all laughed and turned lemons into lemonade. On those days, she would also stay home and they would all do something fun.

Amy Shore agrees that perfection is not the goal—and believes we all need to accept "good enough" from ourselves and others. For a while she criticized her husband's domestic efforts—she told him the laundry wasn't done right, the towels weren't folded right, and he bought the wrong groceries. Finally, her husband had enough and asked, "How would you like it if I followed you around and criticized everything?" From that point on her only words were "thank you."

Keep your eye on the real prize.

As a woman with very high standards, it also wasn't easy for Ally Financial Chief Audit Executive Stephanie Richard to stop sweating the small stuff.

When her husband would help with the laundry, she would secretly refold it to her satisfaction. When her daughter was not mastering potty training right away, Stephanie thought she might have to take a leave of absence from work (until an older neighbor assured her that her daughter would not go off to college in diapers).

Finally, Stephanie realized she had to let go of unnecessary perfection and pay attention to what really matters—raising confident, caring, and happy human beings.

Eliminate the word *should*.

There are many opinions on what working mothers and mothers generally *should* and *should not* do.

Jordana Kammerud tunes out all the distracting noise: "I'm in charge of my own priorities and values."

Cultivate happiness.

Jessica Graziano loves her work, and she loves her life. She always says, "You only have about 80 good years. Don't wait to enjoy your life. Don't get caught up in the minutiae. Feel lucky to have so many great things—your family, your health, your career."

Though this "live in the moment" mantra begs for a gratitude journal, Jessica says, "That's too much work." Instead, she says a quick morning and evening prayer and moves through her day with gratitude in her heart.

Follow the adage "one day at a time."

When you're feeling overwhelmed by work and family responsibilities—and all that needs to be done in the next week, the next month, and a long line of tomorrows—stress can be off the charts.

PPG General Counsel Anne Foulkes says stress will likely ebb and flow, and she advises women to take work and life one day at a time. "You can then stretch it to one week at a time. But worrying about what's farther down the road creates a mental load too heavy to lift."

Give yourself the gift of focus.

Trying to do or think about too many things at once can make it seem like your head will explode. Former Pitney Bowes and current Insulet Chief Financial Officer Ana Maria Chadwick doesn't let that happen.

"I've learned how to hyper-focus—I can be 100 percent at home and 100 percent at work. I don't put unrealistic pressure on myself to be the consummate multitasker. It is freeing—and so much less stressful—to let go and be present."

Ask for a gradual return after maternity leave.

After Joy Corso's first daughter was born, she found it very hard to leave home cold turkey and go back to work full time. When her second daughter was born, she decided to propose a more gradual approach, which her employer embraced. After three weeks home, she went back one day a week, then two days a week, then three days a week, then four days a week—and then eventually she worked up to a full week. This stretched her time at home past the usual three-month maternity leave, got her back to work much sooner, and helped her ease into the separation from her baby—a schedule that had benefits for her family, her own well-being, and her colleagues.

Shannon Lapierre also knows that maternity leave reentry can be hard—especially for first-time mothers. As a result, she tried to be creative about leave programs for women on her team.

One great example: a new mother on her team wasn't ready for her baby to go to daycare—but her mother-in-law agreed to watch the baby two days a week. Shannon said, "Okay, let's start with just two days a week and build on it as you get more comfortable."

"If we had demanded that this new mother immediately work five days a week, we may have lost her. The end game is to keep great talent and show women their employers understand...and care. A phased reentry is definitely something to suggest to your boss."

Hit your motherhood stride over time.

When Jacky Wright's eldest son was young, he would ask her to stay home. She would say she had to work—and point out the nice room he had to play in with fun toys and great books. He would say, "I don't want any of that; I want you."

Through the years, her children became more accepting of her work, largely because she created more quality time they could share. In the early years, she was consumed by work, making sure she could provide for her family. By the time she had her third child she made sure she carved out one-on-one time for each of them every day, even if she was halfway across the world.

Before Jacky traveled internationally for business, she would leave a placemat on the kitchen table that had each country's flag on a map of the world. She put a pin on the places she would visit. Every night she called her daughter at the same time—guiding her through the map and describing each country. In her suitcase she would pack several children's books, and she read them to her daughter over the phone. This ritual gave her daughter the safety of routine, helped her understand where her mother had traveled, and laid the groundwork for a global perspective.

Once when Jacky accompanied her daughter on a class trip to the Bronx Zoo, there were signs to different areas that included country flags. Her daughter saw the flag of India and said to her teacher, "Oh, I know what that flag is... it's India, and my mom went there!"

Jacky now gives younger women the perspective she has built over time. "At some later point you realize you didn't do so badly after all. In the meantime, give yourself grace. It's all a learning process. You're not going to be the perfect mother in the perfect work situation from day one."

"Be focused on creating experiences that will be remembered for a lifetime. You may not be home for every meal or able to go to every sports game. But your kids will remember the special times with you, the things you did often." She knew this was true when many years later her daughter sent her a link to Celine Dion's song "To Love You More." That was a song they played over and over again and danced to when her daughter was a child.

Try not to overcompensate for being a working mother.

When Franklin Templeton Chief Executive Officer Jenny Johnson had children in preschool, she felt compelled to show everyone that despite her career she could send homemade treats to school. Finally, the teacher pulled her aside and said, "Thank you for bringing homemade treats. You're nearly the only mother who does."

Don't overestimate how much time your young children need with you.

When Ryder System Chief Marketing Officer Karen Jones had a son in first grade, she left the workforce to spend more time with him at home. She had been putting in long hours working for Compaq—at the time the fastest-growing company in US history.

The first week she was on hiatus her son ran in the house each day with an exuberant "Hi, Mom!" and lengthy tales of school. The second week it was a quick hello and, "I'm going to Brad's house."

This was Karen's wake-up call that even young children have their own lives. In her opinion, the older your children get, the more they need you. "Children always want your presence and involvement, but their needs and issues are much more complex during the early teenage years. Lots of responsible caregivers can help you change diapers and supervise naps—but the time you really want the most flexibility is later."

Know you can't do everything, but you can do what matters most.

As a mother of four, Ana Maria Chadwick has to tend to many different needs and show each child she's interested and present in their lives. This means she can't possibly be at every school or sports event, but she definitely is there for those her children think are most important.

Ana also gives a little more time to her daughter who has autism. "All children need your love and attention, but sometimes one child needs a little more. I spend a lot of time advocating for my daughter, taking her to adaptive ballet, and helping her move toward the ability to someday have an independent life. I'm open with my other kids about putting in a little extra time with their sister, which makes them appreciate the time I spend with each of them even more."

Don't give in to guilt.

Like many women, Mary Mack felt her share of guilt about being a working mom. Whenever she was feeling particularly stressed, she would look in her sock drawer, where she had saved a "My Hero" story one daughter had written when she was seven. The story began with "My hero is my mom, because she works really hard, but she'll drop everything whenever I need her."

This promise of unconditional communication carried through to later years when her daughter was insistent upon reaching her. First, she called Mary's work phone, then her personal phone, then the work phone again. It so happened that Mary was on stage giving a presentation. By the fourth phone call, Mary thought she had better answer. "Is everything okay?" she asked. Her daughter said yes, but she needed help deciding if she should get a dog.

Mary posed the question to her audience…who all raised their hands in unanimous support.

Play to the seasons in your life.

Among working mothers there's a consensus that "work–life balance" is a flawed notion. Jessica Graziano prefers to think about seasons of life that require extra attention at work or at home.

"Your life and work will never be perfectly balanced. In some seasons you must help a sick relative or get your kids through a pivotal point. Other seasons you have to put extra time into your career. Make your employer part of both your personal and professional journey so they know where you have to put some extra attention."

Don't buy into the idea that more work hours lead to more success.

Former Mercer Chief Executive Officer Martine Ferland says it's important to realize the world will turn without you. Deadlines are deadlines and indeed work must get done, but she believes there are probably very few people on earth who truly need to work 80 or 90 hours a week. "If you find yourself in that situation, you might be in the wrong job."

Martine believes a 24/7 job is not sustainable or healthy. "There are no medals for number of hours worked. One of the ways we can all be leaders is in setting an example for a healthy work–life blend. Leaders need to leave loudly—and show colleagues at all levels that the highest quality work can get done without a crushing, inflexible schedule."

Break free from traditional work norms.

Gregg Renfrew agrees that it's not only a full-time, traditional job that leads to career recognition.

"There's so much power in being clear on your career and financial goals—whatever they may be. A flexible or scaled-down schedule is not necessarily equivalent to less-significant work. If you can remain laser-focused on the things you're working on while balancing personal life realities, that's something to be proud of. It's about output and accomplishments, not hours."

Blend work and life with can-do confidence.

Mastercard's Chief Commercial Payments Officer Raj Seshadri says if you need to slow down...slow down. But try not to stop working altogether. She worked part-time for two years when her children were young.

"Realize you may have more flexibility than you think. In most cases no one is stopping you from leaving for a child's doctor appointment or school play as long as the work gets done. Have confidence. Do what you need to do to be the parent and professional you want to be."

Have it all in a month, not a day.

When people talk about "having it all," it usually refers to being a mother and a professional at the same time. As mentioned earlier, some women say you can have it all, but not at the same time—suggesting that during certain life periods you can choose one or the other…hopefully giving you the chance to experience both over a lifetime.

But Edward Jones Managing Partner Penny Pennington sees it a different way: she assumes women can successfully be both a professional and a mother *all the time*. She knows, though, that having equal work, family, and personal time each day is a tall order.

"So, I look back and say, 'Did I have it all last month? Did I have quality work, family, and personal time over that month, and did it average out to be a reasonable amount of time for each?' No day is going to be a perfect blend of work and life…but a full month can be a good mix of what's important to you and your family."

To avoid feelings of anxiety and defeat, Aon's Global Chief Operating Officer Mindy Simon is even more generous in the time she gives herself to achieve work–life balance.

"It's impossible to be great at all 4 Jobs and equally successful in all your roles—mother, wife, daughter, friend. So I say you can control a year, not a day."

Live by the tenet that quality wins over quantity.

Gregg Renfrew doesn't try to even out the hours she works and the hours she spends with family.

"Quality is far more important than quantity. Thirty minutes of uninterrupted time together will always be better than two hours of time when you're distracted by work or household obligations."

Cut yourself some slack about missing school or sports events.

Anne White, President of Eli Lilly Neuroscience, never missed a parent-teacher conference. But she did have to miss the occasional sports game. "Give yourself some grace. Missing a soccer game doesn't mean you're a bad parent."

She says the most important thing is to truly be present when you are with your kids. "They'll remember that you had your eyes on them throughout the entire games you did attend, not how many games you actually attended."

As a rule, Anne kept the three hours before bedtime as sacred children time, and then when they were in bed she would go back online to prepare for the next day.

On weekends she would keep Saturdays as family time. Then on Sunday afternoons she would tell her kids she had to work for a few hours to get ready for the week. They knew if she did this—if she was more organized—it meant she could preserve her time with them during the week.

Anne's tip is to be proactive in getting school schedules—even before they're published. She would call coaches and school administrators about the dates of key events—tournaments, concerts, field trips. The earlier she could block those days in her calendar, the fewer conflicts she would have with work.

Take pride in all the things you do.

Former Chief Executive Officer of the advertising firm CDM New York turned Executive Coach Sharon Callahan-Miller observes that parents who work professionally tend to get stuck on what they perceive as their parenting failures and shortcomings.

Once as she was apologizing to one of her sons for a lot of recent travel, her son said, "It's okay, Mom, you're here most of the time and when you're here you do a lot for us. Let's not focus on what you haven't done."

Younger children don't always have as much life wisdom. When Raj Seshadri's children would ask why other moms would pick up from school while they were picked up by their nanny, she held strong and wouldn't let guilt creep in.

"Instead, I would tell my kids why I wasn't there and talk about the work I needed to do, just like the schoolwork they needed to do. And I would point out all the many ways I was always present in their lives."

Chapter 14

Put Self-Care on the Top of Your To-Do List

- Be religious about saving time for yourself.
- Teach your kids that self-care is not selfish.
- Keep tweaking your self-care routines.
- Seek out therapy when you need objective advice.
- Don't think of animals as yet another caregiving job.

MOTHERS, OF COURSE, WANT TO help their children and extended families in every way they can. They tend to be overachievers at work—making sure they dot every i and cross every t. And wherever they are, there is a constant loop of household tasks to be done running through their minds.

In most cases, women put themselves last. They simply run out of the time they need to nurture themselves. When you're trying to pack everything into an insanely busy day, exercise can easily fall by the wayside—let alone finding a few minutes to meditate or read a book.

Motherly's annual State of Motherhood report[1] provides a comprehensive view of how women juggle motherhood and their careers. The statistics are alarming: most moms (61 percent) still report getting less than an hour to themselves each day. Very few say they work out every day (11 percent); 35 percent report that they exercise a few times a week on average. This compares to 27 percent who work out a few times a month and 27 percent who exercise a couple of times a year or never.

Particularly notable among the executive women I interviewed for this book is the fact they are the outliers making self-care nonnegotiable. They create *and stick to* routines even though they are raising children to be good citizens of the world and guiding thousands of employees toward personal and company prosperity. The relatively few hours they devote totally to themselves give them the energy and mental health to manage their 4 Jobs.

Be religious about saving time for yourself.

If busy women don't schedule time for themselves, then days, weeks and months will pass with an emphasis on everything and everyone else.

McCann Worldgroup's former Global Chief Product Officer Suzanne Powers knows this all too well. Currently an entrepreneur running her own creativity company, she is religious about keeping an hour for herself every morning between 7:00 and 8:00. During this hour she exercises, meditates, listens to the news, does some casual reading, collects her thoughts—and generally has quiet time to think rationally about various work and life challenges.

"This is sacred me time that helps me power up for the day."

Hormel Foods Chief Financial Officer Jacinth Smiley also schedules her exercise and sticks to it like clockwork—even if her only option is during the wee hours of the morning. At different times in her career, she has gotten up at 3:30 every morning to go to the gym. Her clothes are ready before she goes to sleep and, in her mind, she has a nonnegotiable routine. "When you have a schedule to stick to it's less likely you will back out."

Enlisting exercise buddies is the way that Mutual of Omaha's Chief Administrative Officer Liz Mazzotta keeps herself honest. "It's easy to forego exercise when you're not accountable to anyone else and you have, for example, a treadmill that's easy to ignore in your house. Schedule the nonnegotiable stressbusting, self-care time you need with the support of a group of friends at a gym, on a walk or run, or in a group class."

Unum Group's Chief Investment Officer Martha Leiper credits her exercise consistency to having a variety of options. At her gym she can play tennis, run, cycle, and take many different classes that get her mind and body ready for any stress she'll face later in the day.

Not allowing herself to fall into the "I don't have time" trap, Martha also chooses an early exercise hour—5:00 a.m.—that will not conflict with work or family. "Everyone experiences stress, but not everyone deals with it head-on. You have to find your stress release and continually and consistently let off steam."

Teach your kids that self-care is not selfish.

Women tend to cater to the needs of everyone else—their children, their partners, and, if they are managers, the people on their teams.

When mothers are home, it can seem to be a never-ending stream of "Mom, I need…" or "Mom, where is…" Bath & Body Works President Julie Rosen helps her family just like any other mother, but she also makes it clear she takes care of her own needs, too.

"I make it a point to schedule my exercise, for example—and it may not always be at times that are convenient for my kids. But they have to see the importance of everyone prioritizing their own needs as well as those of others."

Keep tweaking your self-care routines.

JPMorganChase Commercial and Investment Bank Co-Chief Executive Officer, Jennifer Piepszak, admits she hasn't always gotten self-care right. But she's focusing more and more on it as she gets older. Now she prioritizes sleep and exercise. She won't start a meeting before 8:30 a.m., so she has time to exercise, get into the office by 8:00, and get organized for the day.

"You have to really, truly internalize the fact that the most important thing you can do for your family and your job is to take care of yourself."

Seek out therapy when you need objective advice.

Patricia L. Lewis and her wife have a blended family of four children, and meshing two different parenting styles was challenging.

"Communication is everything, and you have to learn to pick your battles. Therapy gives you the ability to see beyond yourself and better understand what others are experiencing."

Don't think of animals as yet another caregiving job.

During the Zoom interview for this book, Liz Mazzotta's cat was slinking between photographs and plants on the credenza in her home office.

"When your work and life are stretching in many different directions, dogs and cats can be stable, quiet, stress-busting companions."

Chapter 15

Foster Independence in Your Children

- Let your kids know they're the most important—but not the only thing in your life.
- Get out of the helicopter.
- Be strategic about giving your kids choices.
- Let your kids follow their own path.

WHEN I WAS GROWING UP, my siblings and I walked out the door after a summer breakfast with a simple "See you later Mom," and we roamed the neighborhood until she rang a bell to call us into dinner. She had no idea where we were or what we were doing—and this laissez-faire approach extended to homework supervision (none), college application help (none), and just the bare minimum of after-school enrichment activities (piano lessons). Mothers of my friends followed about the same routine.

Now many mothers strap themselves into helicopters that monitor their children's activities every minute of every day. Sometimes working mothers who are especially organized direct the lives of their children most of all.

An unfortunate by-product of the helicopter parenting era is a generation of children who often can't make a move without their parents.

I know many mothers who speak to their highly educated children multiple times a day about issues they could easily figure out on their own.

We always want to be sounding boards for our children—but we also want to foster independence and problem-solving skills. The reality is that we live in a world that is less safe and predictable than it used to be, and our children need to be ready to make quick and sound decisions without our carefully orchestrated direction.

In *Raising Kids to Thrive: Balancing Love With Expectations and Protection With Trust*, a book published by the American Academy of Pediatrics, the authors emphasize that a child will never learn life lessons or develop self-reliance if they are protected from experiencing them firsthand.[1]

One of my proudest moments as a mother was the day I dropped my two daughters off at the airport to embark on a trip to Japan. At the time my youngest had just graduated from high school and my oldest was in her early 20s. I held myself back from taking the reins (or getting into their suitcases). They researched and booked a two-week trip to four cities entirely on their own and navigated their way through a country thousands of miles from home. There were some missed trains, times when no one spoke English, and a couple of snafus with hotel reservations, but they figured it all out—drawing from my past encouragement toward independence, not my in-the-moment help.

The key is to give children of any age the space to be resourceful. One CEO told the story of her young daughter, in elementary school, who figured out a school transportation issue on her own. The family had a nanny who didn't drive, but they lived close enough to school for their children to walk. But one day it was raining very hard, and the walk would have left her daughter drenched. Noting the heavy rain, the CEO immediately dove in to help. But when she got her daughter on the phone, she said, "Don't worry, Mom, I called Annie's mother, and she is going to drive me."

There's no question that over-parenting takes up a lot of your life space. Giving your children more independence promotes a bit more freedom all around.

Let kids know that they're the most important— but not the only thing in your life.

JPMorganChase Commercial and Investment Bank Co-Chief Executive Officer Jennifer Piepszak believes it's important for all family members to have independent pursuits—and for her that is work. Mothers and fathers don't accompany kids to school, so she points out to her children that their days are for independent pursuits, too.

Ultimately, she knows her kids understand and are proud of her career. On Mother's Day one son sent her a text: "Happy Mother's Day to the best mom in the world. Instead of driving us to soccer games with a Starbucks coffee mug, you're showing everyone who is boss at a big company."

Jennifer credits that text to her emphasis on quality time. "In this generation parents feel they must cater to their kids 24/7. But if kids know they're your favorite people on the planet, they'll be okay. We can love them wholeheartedly without thinking about their needs every minute of every day."

Get out of the helicopter.

Give most mothers a problem, and they'll immediately try to solve it. That includes the myriad problems that arise as children navigate school, sports, friends, and everything else in their lives.

This "fix it" mentality can endure even when mothers are far from home. Once when Sharon Ryan was on a 20-day business trip in Asia, she discovered the prom dress her daughter ordered online didn't fit. Sharon then spent all night on the phone trying to find the dress in the right size.

"I realized I was always diving in immediately to fix any problem— even with things as simple as making a dentist appointment. In some ways that may have made my daughters more needy—because they tended to figure things out more when my husband and I were less hands-on."

Before you do jump in (and feel the burden of yet another thing on your to-do list), Sharon Callahan-Miller has come to realize the importance of letting her sons do some or all the problem solving (unless they have set the house on fire or broken a leg).

"Whenever my son had an issue, I started thinking about 10 possible solutions. Then I stopped and let him tell me not only how he thought he could solve it, but also how he would be most *comfortable* solving it. Sometimes the solutions we rush toward can actually make a problem worse or somehow cause embarrassment for our kids. Discussing possible solutions really simplified situations and my involvement. Best of all, he felt he owned positive outcomes."

Penny Pennington also sees the value in letting kids figure it out on their own—at least some of the time.

She knows this from her own childhood experience, as the daughter of two working parents in the 70s. Her mother was an executive at a utility company and involved in energy conservation initiatives. When her parents weren't home, Penny always had caregivers to make sure she was safe, but she couldn't run to her mother every five minutes about whatever issues were on her mind.

"I was more independent than many of my friends, and I wanted to keep some space for that personal growth with my daughters, too. I've always encouraged them to think of a couple of possible solutions before they call me for help."

Suzanne Powers takes the same approach: "We have a rule that my sons first try to work out any problem they have—unless it's an emergency or related to health and safety. If they try all possible solutions, then they know they can come to me for help. But I want them to get in the trenches and do the problem solving without me immediately jumping in. Once they come to me, we agree my decision is final—added incentive for them to work things out on their own."

Be strategic about giving your kids choices.

All human beings want some sense of independence—at every age. But too much choice for young children can be a source of parental frustration. Weyerhaeuser Chief Administrative Officer Denise Merle told the story of a colleague who said breakfast time with his son was driving him crazy. The father's question, "What would you like for breakfast?" led them down the black hole of indecision every morning.

"Oh no," Denise said. "You have to limit choices to keep things moving—especially in the morning. Do you want toast—or pancakes? Do you want to wear the red shirt—or the blue shirt?"

When it comes to chores, though—especially for older kids—she says it's a good idea to give them a say on when a task will be done. "Kids have more ownership and responsibility when they feel they have some leeway with a task. The dog has to be fed at the same time every day, but it probably doesn't matter if the grass is cut on Tuesday or Wednesday. Insisting that something is done right away suggests you don't trust it will be done at all."

Denise also learned to have more flexibility with household chores when she asked why her husband had not yet done the laundry. He gently reminded her that "I am in charge of laundry, and it will be done tomorrow—on my timeline, not yours."

Let your kids follow their own path.

Sharon Callahan-Miller knows it can be hard for kids to live up to the success of their parents—especially if your kids really would like to follow an entirely different path. "You can save yourself a lot of stress and angst if you understand that your path is not right for everyone."

Her younger son landed a Division 1 basketball scholarship to a prestigious university and found everyone on the team very seriously gunning for a future spot in the NBA. What had once been a fun passion turned into an overly intense grind. Ultimately, her son decided he didn't want to play basketball anymore—even though he earned the scholar-ship. Sharon's knee-jerk reaction was, "You can't give up. You've been so successful." But she soon realized the only thing that really mattered was her son's happiness. He ultimately found his way to captain of the basket-ball team at a prestigious Division 3 school and is thriving in every way.

Her older son considered following his mother to the corporate world. She helped him get an internship in her field of advertising, think-ing she was putting him on a path to a solid career. At the end of the internship, he evaluated the experience in six words: "I hate sitting at a desk." He said he was more interested in creative pursuits, and today he freelances in television and film production and produces stand-up com-edy on the side.

At first, Sharon expressed her concern: "What about health insur-ance?" But then she stepped back and let him be who he wanted to be—rather than spending a lot of time and energy worrying about who she thought he should be. (And like many other freelancers, he does have health insurance and the freedom of not sitting at just one desk.)

Chapter 16

Find Caregivers Who Are Parenting Partners

- Don't assume your kids will be unhappy at daycare.
- Ask if you can bend the daycare rules.
- See caregivers as a window to the world.
- Give your children the opportunity to form many family bonds.
- Minimize childcare through school resources.
- Look for caregivers who care about their reputation.
- Use your business skills to interview prospective caregivers.
- Zero in on caregiver values.
- Don't immediately trust a rave review.
- Choose a caregiver who will co-parent.
- Look for an honest and open caregiving partner.
- Search for the #1 attribute most important to your family.
- Consider an older caregiver who can help you learn the ropes.
- Ask a potential caregiver the "what-ifs."
- Try to meet a prospective caregiver's family.
- Look for grit, work ethic, and a loving nature.
- Weed out caregivers looking for a stop-gap job.
- Evaluate if caregivers will adapt to your evolving family needs.
- Pay a little bit more so your childcare is not a revolving door.
- Consider childcare an investment in the whole family.

- Don't assume caregivers are on the same page.
- Create a working agreement for all caregivers—even if they are family.
- Look for caregivers you can help, too.
- Give your child's caregiver the work–life perks you want yourself.
- If you make a caregiver mistake, cut bait quickly.
- Think of childcare as a support network.

I ALWAYS SAY THE HARDEST PART of working is not the work... it's finding safe, reliable, and reasonably priced childcare that fits your budget and your family's needs.

Interestingly, many of the C-suite women I interviewed for this book had in-home childcare providers who stayed with their families (and essentially *became* family) for many years. Part of this is just luck, but they tipped good fortune in their favor through a business approach to finding, screening, and hiring candidates.

Though I set out to be extremely careful in hiring caregivers, I experienced my fair share of mistakes. These executive women also have had a no-nonsense business process for correcting mistakes—they make a change firmly and *swiftly*. In retrospect, I sometimes waited too long, hoping that a less than ideal nanny would miraculously change and eventually work out.

Without a doubt, when you know, you know. The nannies who did not work out for my family were the ones I made a few excuses for in the hiring process. Maybe this or that shortcoming wouldn't be such a big deal. But they were, and I could have avoided a lot of stress for both me and my daughters by listening to my gut from the start.

Even the best caregivers, however, may not eliminate an issue that I struggled with on my own and I see jeopardizing the work lives of my coaching clients. It's that pesky motherhood guilt about not spending enough time with your children. Or wrestling with the unfounded idea (often planted in your mind by a judgmental non-working family member or friend) that you're letting someone else raise your children.

The women in this chapter make it clear caregivers help *you* raise your children. They emphasize the depth of bonds with your children—measured in your visible caring and interest in their lives—not in the number of hours you are face-to-face.

Don't assume your children will be unhappy at daycare.

For a few years, Liz Mazzotta needed daycare options for her preschool daughter. But she initially worried her daughter would be upset when she dropped her off and left.

She found the opposite was true.

When Liz dropped her daughter off, she was perfectly happy. Each day when she returned at pickup time, her daughter would look at her and say, "Why are you here so early? Can I stay longer?"

"The benefit of daycare is that many kids prefer the interaction with other kids rather than being home alone with a nanny."

Ask if you can bend the daycare rules.

Although most daycare centers can be very rigid about their hours, when Jordana Kammerud was a single parent, she was successful in getting special accommodations for an earlier drop-off time.

"What daycare professionals don't want is parents who continually expect that it's okay not to follow guidelines. If you're respectful of the rules and upfront about your needs, they'll usually work with you."

See caregivers as a window to the world.

Mastercard's Chief Commercial Payments Officer Raj Seshadri employed the same nanny, who was like a grandmother, from the time her children were young until they were in high school. And she hired a variety of au pairs for several years. These women came from all over the world—Jamaica, Germany, Namibia, Mexico, Costa Rica, and Columbia.

"All these caregivers gave my sons a world perspective far beyond our home. They learned to speak Spanish, understood the differences among cultures, and even spent time with their families."

Give your children the opportunity to form many family bonds.

Karen Jones believes mothers should consider the many family members who can be part of school and extracurricular activities.

"It's not all on you as the mother to be interested and present. It's equally important that children bond with your spouse or partner, nearby grandparents, and other family members. A parent doesn't have to be at every baseball game. My husband and I always made sure someone was present—and sometimes it was my mother. Make room for your children to form other family bonds."

Minimize childcare through school resources.

When Liz Mazzotta and her husband had young children, they were strategic about childcare. For the most part, they could minimize their need for caregivers by taking advantage of school resources.

A Montessori school had an all-day program starting at age 18 months. An elementary school had an after-school enrichment program until 6:00 p.m. Both she and her husband were always able to work full days and switch off on drop-offs and pickups.

"Aside from the fact that you save money, there's a lot of safety in programs linked to schools. You can't always fully vet the caregivers you hire. But schools typically screen all hires comprehensively to ensure expertise and safety."

Look for caregivers who care about their reputation.

Many parents find it difficult to hire a total stranger to care for their children. Weyerhaeuser Chief Administrative Officer Denise Merle always tried to hire caregivers who had a mutual connection and a reason for their reputation to be on the line.

Once she hired one of the teachers her children had in preschool. Another time she hired a nanny from the neighborhood when the family that nanny was working for relocated.

"Choose caregivers who have their own value system to do the best job possible—but also those who don't want to let down your mutual connections."

Use your business skills to interview prospective caregivers.

Before I interviewed former Chief Executive Officer of CBRE's Global Workplace Solutions business, Chandra Dhandapani, for this book, she read a list of questions I would likely ask. She told me she teared up when she remembered how hard it was to manage childcare throughout her career.

When she first brought her son to a traditional daycare facility, he cried—and so did she. Though they both could have gotten over the separation anxiety, the fact that he was constantly sick cut the arrangement short. Her pediatrician then recommended a woman who cared for just a few children in her home.

To make sure that this woman (and subsequent others Chandra hired) was the right caregiver for her son, she made a list of everything she wanted to learn in the conversation—as she did when she prepared to interview candidates for business roles. She asked caregivers and business candidates similar questions, such as these:

- Will this caregiver get on the floor and play with my child? (Similar to: Will this professional get into the nitty-gritty of business projects?)

- Does this caregiver seem overly chatty—someone who might spend a lot of time on the phone, rather than playing with my child? (Similar to: Will this professional be too social in the office—not focused enough on work and prone to distracting others?)
- Will this caregiver be aware—a good listener who has sound intuition—with the ability to quickly see and hear that my child has a problem? (Similar to: Will this professional not get lost in the mundane and realize right away that a problem needs to be addressed and averted?)

"In the end, your relationship with a caregiver is a business relationship. For a lot of the skills you look for in a professional candidate, there is a parallel in a caregiver candidate. Honesty and kindness are important, but you also want to be sure they will fundamentally be a good employee."

Zero in on caregiver values.

When Suzanne Powers interviews candidates for a professional job, she asks all the normal questions about skills and experience. But what she really wants to get at are the person's sense of values and beliefs—generally what makes them tick. This approach carried over to her conversations with potential caregivers.

"During any interview I want to find out if candidates are curious, if they are learners. In caregivers, I wanted to see if they sought to understand humans, if they studied education, or if they had an interest in different cultures. Ultimately, you should trust your instincts, but I always looked for shared interests, too. One of our best nannies loved Harry Potter as much as our sons did."

Don't immediately trust a rave review.

When Gregg Renfrew was in the market for childcare, she reached out to her personal network.

"A recommendation from a friend is always best. Then do your own research about the person your friend recommends, but also trust your gut. If you sense something is off, even if you have gotten rave reviews, the person just may not be the right fit for your children."

Choose a caregiver who will co-parent.

A Chief Executive Officer in the beauty industry considers her son's full-time caretaker a third parent—one of the reasons the caretaker has stayed with their family for eight years. "Part of it is just luck, but after interviewing lots of candidates I could see my son responding to her in a very special way."

Over the years, she has made peace with the fact that the caretaker spends as much—and sometimes more time—with her son each week. Like many mothers, she worries about time away from her son, but she truly believes she is sharing, not relinquishing, her parenting role.

"Make room in your heart and mind for this third parent—and realize your child is actually lucky to have another person who loves and cares for him the way we do. Who wouldn't want more love?"

Gregg Renfrew acknowledges finding the right childcare is the first critical step. But she knows *keeping* the right childcare is equally important. "Treat caregivers as partners and work in lockstep with them in all areas of your children's lives, so all interactions with your children are seamless. Longstanding relationships with your family are most likely to happen when you treat them with the respect they deserve."

Look for an open and honest caregiving partner.

When her two sons were young, Sharon Callahan-Miller was a single mother. She wanted the caregivers she hired to feel like they were part of her family—and she worked hard to create a partnership that would benefit her sons.

In a true partnership, you invite open and honest communication. One longtime housekeeper (Shawna, who is still an extended family member) asked if she could speak to Sharon about some concerns. At the time her sons were 15 and 10.

"I know you have a lot of responsibility at work," Shawna began. "You travel a lot, and you don't have a lot of time. But you can't be the way you are at work when you're at home."

Shawna observed Sharon bringing her work efficiency to the household—pushing to get things done without taking the time to truly connect to the lives of her boys. This constructive criticism was a turning point for Sharon—when she vowed to spend more time on the human side of parenting and running a household, rather than just getting through a daily to-do list.

This realization carried over to Sharon's work. "I realized my employees might also be seeing me only as a driven executive laser-focused on work. As a true partner, Shawna showed me I needed to show up with more love at home and more caring at work."

Search for the #1 attribute most important to your family.

Of course, lots of caregivers have many good qualities, observes Joy Corso. "But do they have that one quality that helps you sleep at night?"

In Joy's case she wanted and searched for stability in caregivers... and with that she also found dependability, maturity, and responsibility.

Consider an older caregiver who can help you learn the ropes.

For Jonita Wilson's first child, she found great in-home daycare through "Mama Kathy," who treated her son like her own grandson.

She knew Mama Kathy was the right caregiver from the moment the potential caregiver walked into her home. There was an obvious and authentic connection—and Mama Kathy immediately engaged with Jonita's son.

There was also a strong connection with Jonita, who could tell that Mama Kathy was an experienced mother she could learn from. "I was 27 when my first son was born and there was a lot I didn't know and no manual to turn to. Mama Kathy was my motherhood manual."

Ask a potential caregiver the "what-ifs."

When Ocean Spray Chief Commercial Officer Monisha Dabek hired caregivers, she always looked for those who had children of their own. She also screened for safety and accountability—and made sure they seemed warm and caring.

Then she looked for resourcefulness. "I wanted to be sure caregivers would have the intelligence, tenacity, and experience to figure things out. I asked, for example, the first three things they would do if my child had a fever. Hearing the steps they would take gave me a clear idea of how they think and how quickly they would take real action."

Try to meet a prospective caregiver's family.

It just so happened a prospective nanny former Deere & Company General Counsel Mary Jones found on Care.com was driven to the interview by her mother. When Mary found out the mother was waiting in the car, she invited her in. This was a big bonus—seeing how the caregiver interacted with her mother and getting a glimpse into her upbringing.

Though it would probably be difficult (and unheard of) to ask a prospective caregiver to bring a family member to an interview, Mary's story reminded me of a mother who had a similar idea. This mother would interview a caregiver in her home, and then ask to drop by the caregiver's home for a second interview. This provided an opportunity to see how the caregiver lived (mainly in terms of organization), and perhaps meet a husband or children to get some insight into their family life. Many people believe when you hire someone who will work in your home, you're essentially hiring their families, too.

In Mary's case, she also looked for caregivers who had a calling for helping people. She hired the caregiver who brought her mother along—and liked the fact that she was studying to be an occupational therapist.

Look for grit, work ethic, and a loving nature.

Jennifer Piepszak's family had a live-in nanny from Brazil for 10 years whom they found through a student-exchange program.

The young woman gave Jennifer a big hug when she walked in the door to her interview, so she immediately checked the warmth box. Then Jennifer commented that the nanny spoke English very well. She had only spent one year in the United States with another family and could barely speak English when she arrived. To quickly learn how to converse well, she forced herself to hang out only with nannies from English-speaking countries so she could immerse herself in the language. That showed Jennifer the grit and willingness to work hard she could expect the nanny to have on the job.

Weed out caregivers looking for a stop-gap job.

One live-out nanny who BET Networks Chief Marketing Officer Kimberly Paige hired stayed with her family for eight years—and her children had only three nannies throughout their childhood.

Kimberly credits the long tenure of their nannies to her careful screening process. "I wanted to hire nannies who were looking to work with children as a life calling, not a stop gap before a completely different career."

She met one of her long-term nannies at a nursery school—a woman who had a degree in early childhood education. "I knew she had a true passion to nurture children."

Evaluate if caregivers will adapt to your evolving family needs.

When mothers hire a caregiver, they look most of all for someone trustworthy who can keep their children safe. Then there are a range of other responsibilities they may want the caregiver to handle: driving to school and activities, supervising playdates, doing laundry, running errands, making dinner, and more.

Over the 25 years a nanny worked for Mary Mack's family, she had many roles. She was hired as a baby nurse, but later was more of an after-school babysitter—and filled in with many household needs, such as cooking, grocery shopping, and laundry.

"Think ahead about how your family's needs will change over the next six months, two years, and longer. A more flexible and adaptable nanny is likely to stay with you through many of your children's ages and stages—and essentially become part of your family."

Pay a little bit more so your childcare is not a revolving door.

Insulet Chief Financial Officer Ana Maria Chadwick often hears women talk about how to find the least expensive childcare. But her advice is to pay a bit more—to really invest in the person who will be caring for your children.

Her theory has merit since her family had the same caregiver for 19 years. "Paying well shows the caregiver respect as a professional. Then if you treat caregivers like family, involve them in decisions, bring them on vacations—you develop trust and loyalty. You can't look for a bargain when caregivers are your invaluable eyes and ears. Pay up for the people who will take the best care of your treasures."

Consider childcare an investment in the whole family.

When working mothers choose limited childcare, there are often gaps that make it necessary for everyone in the family to miss out on various activities. It could be it's not possible for a caregiver to take a toddler to an afternoon music class if an older child needs to be picked up from sports. Or there might not be an exercise class when a mother has coverage.

That's why Jill Penrose leaned into full-time childcare, including early morning and evening coverage.

"I spent a disproportionate amount on childcare, but it was worth it for the peace of mind. I had very long workdays, and my husband was traveling extensively so we really needed the full coverage. I saw it as an investment in the whole family's needs and scheduling options and put off things like home renovations and big vacations."

Don't assume caregivers are on the same page.

Though Sharon Ryan knew the value of experienced caregivers, one incident showed her she needed to be very explicit about the way she and her husband wanted to raise their daughters.

Sharon found out one day that a caregiver was using something resembling a fly swatter to enforce discipline. The woman would swat Sharon's children lightly on the leg if they did something she didn't like—which was counter to the fact Sharon and her husband didn't believe in any form of spanking.

When she confronted the older caregiver about her method of discipline, Sharon was met with some resistance. She found that caregivers who have raised their own children could be set in their ways, and she ultimately favored younger caregivers whom she found less rigid.

Create a working agreement for all caregivers—even if they are family.

When former Sysco Chief Supply Chain Officer Marie Robinson was a single divorced mother, her parents took early retirement to help with the care of her sons. They moved with her to two different states and lived in her home for five years.

While Marie is extremely appreciative her parents gave her family this gift of their time and care, she wishes she had set better rules and boundaries. When she would come home from a long day, she wanted to decompress and spend quiet time with her boys, but her parents were always right there expecting attention, too.

"There is still a need for guidelines even when the caregiver is family—especially when it comes to advice about how things should be done. It can't always be your way or their way—just as in any other working arrangement, you need to discuss and reach agreement."

Marie learned this when she later hired a nanny through an agency that suggested a working agreement to manage expectations on both sides and cultivate a true partnership. Over time they revisited the working agreement, and there was always open communication about what was fair and equitable—probably the reason the nanny stayed with her family for eight years.

Look for caregivers you can help, too.

Patricia L. Lewis was a divorced single parent for many years, and when her son was young, she hired a family friend as a live-in nanny. They formed a very special relationship that went beyond employer-employee.

The nanny helped Patricia care for her son and keep on top of school and extracurricular activities. In turn she helped the nanny leave her parents' home, move from the West to East Coast, and generally get on her feet. There was tremendous mutual respect and appreciation for the help they gave each other—and Patricia was also a professional role model for the nanny, who eventually earned her nursing degree. To this day they remain friends.

Give your child's caregiver the work–life perks you want yourself.

Women who work in corporate settings aren't the only ones craving a better work–life balance. Every woman in every job needs to find ways to blend work and life.

When Joy Corso's family had a live-out nanny, the woman needed an afternoon babysitter for her own child. They allowed the nanny's daughter to take the bus after school to their home—where she played with Joy's young daughters, did her homework, and stayed within her mother's sight.

This gave Joy's daughters a chance to interact with an older child and saved the nanny from a time-consuming school pickup and expensive after-school care. Paying attention to the nanny's well-being created a special bond that led to three years of employment.

If you make a caregiver mistake, cut bait quickly.

Even the most cautious parents can hire the wrong caregiver. Though I used reputable agencies, checked many references, got referrals from friends, and did everything I could to make sure the person I was hiring was honest, dependable, and truly caring, I made a couple of hiring mistakes myself.

I agree with Joy: It doesn't take weeks to figure out a caregiver is not the right fit. Joy says "Very quickly you just know, and your kids know. We had a nanny for just one week once and our daughters reacted badly to her. I also felt something was off, and I hadn't seen it in the interview. My instinct said it wasn't something we could wait out, and we made a quick change."

But making a change isn't always easy. Starting the interviewing process again when you're stretched to the limit at work and home can cause many mothers to give caregivers a longer trial period and hope things level out. Joy says it's better to tell your boss you're in-between caregivers and ask for some schedule flexibility—rather than jeopardize the safety of your kids.

When I found out an afterschool babysitter I shared with another mother had left our five-year-olds alone in the car in the middle of traffic to yell at another driver who had cut her off, we fired her the same day.

You can make a mistake with daycare facilities, too. Marie Robinson says appearances can be deceiving. "A nice building or a brand-new facility does not necessarily equal the best care. Dig deeper to make sure there are baseline safety and fundamental practices aligning with your values. Do a lot of research—talk to people in and outside of the facility until your gut tells you it's right. And if you make a mistake, move on knowing you've learned new questions to ask."

Think of childcare as a support network.

Even if you have a live-in nanny, you will have to contend with sick days. Smita Pillai points out you can't rely on just one person. "You need to purposefully develop a mutual support system with friends, neighbors, teachers, babysitters, and family. The more people you have in your network, the more coverage you have for any unanticipated situation."

When you're building your network, Smita says it's important to respect the time of stay-at-home moms. Don't assume they have unlimited, unstructured time. She learned this lesson when her son's teacher said he needed to interact more in the classroom. She wasn't quite sure how to make opportunities for him to do so. So she enlisted the help of a neighbor, a stay-at-home-mom who suggested they meet at 2:00 p.m. for coffee. Smita's natural inclination was to ask if they could meet after her workday, but instead she moved her calendar around so she could meet in the middle of the day. Respecting the neighbor's time has solidified their relationship and willingness to help each other out.

Chapter 17

Connect Your Children to Both Your Work and Life

- Help your children understand what you do at that place called "work."
- Be a role model.
- Look at the big-picture ways your job benefits your children.
- Play dolls and play work.
- Take your children to work.
- Tell stories that bring your colleagues to life.
- Describe your workday with almost 100% candor.
- Show it takes hard work to be a mother and a professional.
- Let your children know what it took to get where you are.
- Look for work–life teaching moments.
- Make your kids part of the big world, too.
- Don't sugarcoat the tough stuff.
- Admit work-life mistakes.
- Share to promote sharing.
- Find a role for your kids in your work life.
- Show how your work can make a difference for your family—and the world.
- Give children some control of your schedule.

- Let kids be part of big family decisions.
- Talk to your older kids about what it was really like to have a working mother.

THOUGH SUSPENDING OR ENDING MY career never entered my mind, as mentioned earlier I did a fair amount of worrying that my choice to work was somehow alienating my children. Perhaps the best evidence to the contrary: a drawing my daughter gave me when she was about five. In the picture she drew I was working at my desktop computer. Next to me my daughter was coloring, and next to her was the dog.

In so many ways my daughters have been a part of my work life. I was fortunate to have many flexible work situations (well before the pandemic), and I often brought my daughters to my office. This gave them the chance to clearly see where I worked. They saw me in action, and they heard the conversations I had with colleagues. They knew the basics: I was helping women find jobs, I was planning conferences lots of people would attend, I was writing books. And they got to know and formed relationships with my colleagues: one woman I worked with had a photo of my daughter prominently displayed in her home.

Like me, the executive women who contributed to this chapter didn't compartmentalize their lives. They made sure their children understood what they did at work and why it was important to their families and the greater world.

Help your children understand what you do at that place called "work."

Younger children often don't get the fuzzy concept of work and wonder what their parents do that takes them away from home all day. During the pandemic, when many parents worked at home, one child was asked what kind of job his mother had, and he said with a full dose of disinterest,

"She works on the computer and talks on the phone." Through this lens, work looks like about as much fun as cleaning your room.

To give more color to what your work involves and why you like doing it, relate your job to something tangible. A finance job is about money. A pharmaceutical job is about making medicine for sick people. A lawyer helps people follow rules.

Working for a company that has familiar products is easier for a young child to grasp, and one Chief Executive Officer in the beauty industry made a point of showing her son her company's products on store shelves.

"During the pandemic, when we were all working at home, I would get deliveries of products to test, and my young son would always be interested to see what was in the box. He saw how excited I was about the products. Most of all, he saw that a job is interesting and fun—and he felt a part of it."

The best way to be a professional role model for your kids, suggests Liz Mazzotta, is to indeed let them see the pleasure you get from your work. "Show them you love your family, and you love your work. Let them see the discipline and dedication of working day in and day out for something productive you really enjoy. I always loved 'Take Your Children to Work' day, which in our company was offered to 12-year-olds. It was a full day of well-planned experiences, including live animals as part of Mutual of Omaha's Wild Kingdom branding."

Be a role model.

Working mothers may be away from their children many hours a day, but their children are always watching and listening.

As Karen Jones's son was growing up, he always said, "My mom is my business hero. I want to be just like her." It helped that as Chief Marketing Officer for a major company she was also responsible for sports marketing. Her son benefited from the "cool factor" of her job—getting great seats at lots of football and baseball games the company sponsored.

Now, after all the years of watching his mother, Karen's son, now in his 30s, has also established a career in sports marketing.

Look at the big-picture ways your job benefits your children.

When Denise Merle was in the thick of building a career and raising young children, she sometimes worried about missing the occasional school event. This was the case when she had to travel for a board meeting, and she was not able to attend her son's kindergarten graduation.

Denise's husband and her sister were there, and they made sure her son had a special day. She knew she was overthinking that one absence: "Since I made sure to attend as many events as possible, I'm sure my son never thought twice about it."

Years later, Denise realizes her work continually added to—not subtracted from—her children's lives. "I was so worried about missing a sports game that would soon fade from everyone's memory. What was really lasting—what my kids never forgot—was everything my work taught them about providing for a family, leading people, a strong work ethic, and critical thinking."

For her daughter, especially, watching Denise be a strong mother and a strong professional has been the impetus for her own intention—as a chemist—to work and raise a family.

Play dolls and play work.

When her children were young, Mary Mack always made it a point to talk about her work, describe her office, and give her kids a mental picture of who she spent time with every day.

She knew they were catching on to what it means to work in an office when they would ask her to play "meeting" in their living room...passing each other notecards and talking on imaginary phones.

Take your children to work.

On days off from school, Shannon Lapierre would bring her daughter to work, where she would give her little projects to do, take her to lunch in the cafeteria, and let her play "adult" for the day. She also took her to the company's philanthropic events—walk-a-thons and fundraisers.

Shannon's daughter loved getting dressed up to "go to work", and through the years it was a way for her to get to know her mother's colleagues. It was very intentional: Shannon wanted her colleagues to be visible to her daughter, and she wanted her daughter to be visible to her colleagues.

"I always said, when you work on my team you get my husband, my daughter, and my dog."

Sharon Ryan also wanted her daughters to build relationships with colleagues. When she created fun office events around holidays—like Halloween, Thanksgiving, or the Super Bowl—she brought her daughter to the office.

On random days Sharon also brought her daughters in—they loved the hot chocolate machine and the bowls of candy on different desks. Her daughters knew she was a lawyer (and had some understanding of the profession from TV), but Sharon was most concerned that her daughters could see her having fun and enjoying interactions with lots of different people in her office.

Tell stories that bring your colleagues to life.

With more and more remote work, it's not always possible to bring your children to the office. But they can feel like they know more about your colleagues in other ways.

Ally Financial Chief Audit Executive Stephanie Richard has always told stories about her colleagues by name. Her kids expected to hear about Brian, Linda, and others—and the different projects they worked on. It was the same as Stephanie hearing about the kids at school.

"To make my work more real and tangible, I would show them ads our company created and explain that we help people save money to buy a house. This made them feel part of the company, too—and proud of my work."

Describe your workday with almost 100% candor.

When you come home to your family, Anne White says you can certainly be honest about being very busy or stressed on a deadline—but you don't want to make it seem like day after day you can't stand your job.

"An ongoing negative attitude about your job can confuse kids. They'll wonder why you're away from them doing something that makes you unhappy."

Show it takes hard work to be a mother and a professional.

At one point in Anne Foulkes's career, she had to travel to Brazil three times a year. When she arrived home after one particularly challenging trip, she sat on her front porch and cried. She had always tried to shield her daughters from the tough parts of blending work and life but realized that occasionally it was okay for her daughters to see the underside—the not-so-rosy aspects of providing support for the family.

"It's important for your children to understand that the work we do away from them is not fun and games—we're working hard to bring financial rewards home."

Though professional work poses many challenges, Anne also talks to her daughters about the benefits of hard work. She believes being a mother and a professional makes you better at each role.

Let your children know what it took to get where you are.

Every year, Jacinth Smiley brings her son back to the village where she grew up in Jamaica, which has unpaved roads and no running water. "Give your children a clear picture of your life and work journey and all the bumps along the way."

Jacinth's mother brought her to the United States and cleaned houses to support her family. Jacinth worked at McDonald's during college. "Through your stories your children see how they can work hard, persevere, support their families, and get to an admirable place."

Look for work–life teaching moments.

When Jill Penrose's son said, "You work all the time," it was during a particularly busy period when she had to work even when she was home.

"I saw this as a teaching moment...when I explained I had to work extra time to prepare for an upcoming board meeting. We talked about the difference between working all the time or working to prepare for something big. I compared it to the times when he had a test coming up and had to work extra hard."

Make your kids part of the big world, too.

Children orbit a relatively small world between home and daycare or school. In comparison, when their mothers are not working remotely, it seems like they're going off into a bigger, harder-to-imagine world. Tonit Calaway always looked for ways to broaden her kids' horizons so they would have more of an understanding of the world where she worked and traveled.

Raising her children with a sense of adventure, she brought them to restaurants, to movies, and on long trips when they were very young. From their home in the Midwest, they traveled to New York City often—seeing lots of Broadway plays. When Tonit wasn't home, her children knew she was out working in that big world they felt they were part of, too.

Jennifer Piepszak also tried to draw her children into her work travel. "Whenever I called during a business trip, I seized the opportunity to talk about the city I was in, the culture, the food, and the interesting people I met. By doing this, they were less concerned about me being away, and more a part of my experience."

Don't sugarcoat the tough stuff.

Three years into her marriage to Mike Fidler, Penny Pennington found out she had breast cancer. This was frightening for her, but especially difficult for her husband's young daughters, then ages seven and nine, who had recently lost their own mother to cancer.

"First, I promised I wasn't going to die, which, given my diagnosis, my doctor assured me was true. Then I didn't hide any of the hard stuff from them—they knew when I was uncomfortable or tired, but they also knew I was very optimistic. I didn't treat them like babies, and without saying the words, through my actions I asked them to grow up a little and help me through a difficult time both at work and at home. They saw many others helping me—friends, colleagues, and clients—and they wanted to help, too."

Admit work-life mistakes.

There was a two-year period when Allstate Chief Legal Officer Christine DeBiase was head down, totally engulfed by work. At the time, her previous company was going public, and she was given major responsibilities—and a huge career opportunity—to make it all happen without a hitch.

Christine's family was then living in North Carolina, and she had to spend four days a week in New York City. Her wife gave up her job and essentially became a single parent—and her daughter and son didn't see Christine for long stretches of time.

She remembers a day when she walked out of her bedroom with a suitcase. Her daughter saw the suitcase, quickly darted into her room, and slammed the door behind her. Christine finally faced the fact that her absences were hurting her daughter and made it a priority to address her feelings.

"I didn't try to defend myself—instead I explained why my work required me to be away so much. I validated her feelings and acknowledged just how hard it had been on her and the entire family. Admitting I hadn't addressed her feelings earlier made it easier for my daughter to understand the situation but did not take away the hurt. In the years since, I've had to show her—not just tell her—I'd never take our family for granted again."

Share to promote sharing.

When Aon Global Chief Operating Officer Mindy Simon shares information about her day, she finds her kids are more apt to open up and share, too.

"Instead of just asking about their day, which usually does not elicit a big response, I'll first tell them, for example that mine was okay because I was working on a really difficult project. That opens the door to more conversation."

Find a role for your kids in your work life.

Chandra Dhandapani always tries to involve her teenage son in her work life. In one area her son has been a valued adviser. Chandra has to speak to large groups often, and her son draws on his gift for public speaking to help her prepare.

When Chandra has a big presentation coming up, she practices with her son, and he has been able to give her some great suggestions about pacing her remarks or using more conversational language.

Show how your work can make a difference for your family—and the world.

Mothers tell their children they earn money to help the family with all kinds of living expenses—and the fun things like vacations. But children don't often know the less obvious reasons a mother's work can make a difference in the world.

Christine DeBiase is in a same-sex marriage, and she tells her children that her stature in the business world gives her a platform to advocate for LGBTQ+ family rights.

"There are not a lot of women in the C-suite, and my position affords me many opportunities to speak to professional and community groups about issues that matter to our family."

Give children some control of your schedule.

When Mary Mack's daughters were in high school, she had to do a lot more overnight travel.

Her family had a meeting to discuss what her absences would mean for the family—and she asked her daughters what they would need. As an example, she made a calendar of one daughter's volleyball games and asked when it would be really important for Mary to attend. She promised she wouldn't miss a single one of those deemed most important and she would never miss two games in a row. This gave her daughter a sense of control: "She told me when I didn't need to be there, rather than me just not showing up."

Penny Pennington not only tried to zero in on the school events her daughters felt were most important, but she also asked them to weigh the relative importance of each event. Going through the school calendar she would ask questions like "Is it more important for me to be home early to celebrate your birthday or be at your birthday celebration at school?"

"Through conversations that have this level of detail, kids know they have your love and attention. With that foundation, they will be okay if you can't be with them 100 percent of the time."

Let kids be part of big family decisions.

Women usually discuss life and work decisions with their husband or partner. Less frequently they involve their young children in big decision making.

Suzanne Powers has always had a "we're all in this together" approach. Whenever the family was in the market for a new apartment, her twin sons weighed in about which one they liked best. Or when Suzanne was interviewing for a new position, she discussed all the interviews and the opportunities each job offered.

"I treat my sons like partners in my work and life, which makes them feel valued and included."

Talk to your older kids about what it was really like to have a working mother.

Few working mothers can totally escape even fleeting feelings of guilt.

Kris Malkoski told her adult daughter she sometimes feels guilty she was not around more when she was growing up. "I know when you went to Cindy's house, her mom was always there."

Her daughter quickly dismissed the idea that Kris's career had a negative impact on her. "Mom, whenever you were with me, you were totally present—not cleaning the house or talking to friends on the phone."

Chapter 18

Be There When You Can't Be There

- Remember that wherever you are, your kids can see your heart.
- Say "I wish I could be there" instead of "I can't be there."
- Keep routines with your children when you're away on business.
- Use technology to be in the room.
- Know there's room in your schedule for school events that matter most.

THROUGHOUT MY CAREER, I, THANKFULLY, had to do only occasional business travel. But when I did need to be away for a night or more, I made sure my daughters felt my presence—even when I was several states away.

Like the many executive women I interviewed, daily check-in calls were routine. Then I found everyone has had their own special ways of making their young children feel they were not far away. In my case, I bought a lot of greeting cards and wrote funny little notes my daughters could open and read throughout their days.

Separation from your children starts when they go off to school for the first time. Then when they go to college, another phase begins when you will not see them for long stretches of time. They come home for some, but not all, school vacations and summer breaks. Then they graduate and move into their own apartments—sometimes in cities far away from home.

But all the women I interviewed described stronger and stronger bonds with each milestone that marked more separation. You can't be with your children every minute, but these women found ways for their children to always feel their love and support.

Remember that wherever you are, your kids can see your heart.

If magic was possible, working mothers would choose to be in two places at once. Former Chief Executive Officer of Voya Investment Management Christine Hurtsellers raised a son who understood she was both a good mom and a good professional. He recalled she was not at every minor school function, but she was always there for him when it mattered.

"I'm incredibly proud of you, Mom," he said. "You've been a great role model. I saw a lot of other kids who were overmanaged, and I'm grateful for the freedom and independence you gave us."

Wherever Christine was, she relied on a strong connection with each of her six boys. "Whether I'm in the same house or in another country, my kids have the foundation that 'I see you,' 'I love you,' and 'I'm here for you.'"

Jenny Johnson agrees we all need to get over any guilt we feel about working. One way to do that, she says, is to blend work and life so daughters, nieces, and other young women will see it's indeed possible—and pleasurable—to do so. "Sometimes life takes precedence, and sometimes work is a higher priority. It's about putting it into perspective by asking yourself which individual event or task will be more important when looking back in five years."

Both Jenny and Christine believe all women can work and raise happy, well-adjusted children—even when they have big families. Like Christine, Jenny has many children (five), and Jenny's mother had seven. At a time when many women were not working outside of the home, Jenny's mother went back to school after having children and graduated from Stanford Medical School, eventually nurturing both patients and her family.

Say "I wish I could be there" instead of "I can't be there."

Children often hear working parents say "I can't" do this or that because of work. Jennifer Piepszak always made it clear she would love to be there, but she had other responsibilities.

In one of her son's grades there was a tight group of mothers, many of whom didn't work...or if they did, they worked locally or with reasonable hours. This group of moms often went on overnight trips or did fun things as a group with their sons.

"I made up for it by making ours the 'boy house' and having lots of gatherings on weekends."

Keep routines with your children when you're away on business.

When mothers travel, family routines are interrupted and children can feel out of synch with their parents.

Despite an extensive travel schedule and many different time zones, a C-suite woman I once met told me she made sure to speak to her son at the same time every day...just before he went to sleep. This often meant she had to excuse herself from a business meeting.

This executive's son knew to expect this daily call from his mother. While her colleagues discussed business without her for 10 minutes, she sang the same favorite song to her son—shortening the miles between them and giving them both closure for the day.

Mindy Simon says keeping routines in her family means never missing what they call the "kiss and a hug" chant. At every bedtime and every morning when they get out of bed—even by phone when Mindy is away—she recites the "kiss and a hug" with each child (which sounds a bit like a pep rally), and they end with a high five.

Use technology to be in the room.

At different times during Chandra Dhandapani's career she needed to travel overnight frequently, but she tried not to stay away for more than two nights. The international trips were the hardest, and she did everything she could to stay "present" in her son's life when she was away—FaceTiming when he got up, when he got home from school, and before bedtime.

As Chandra's son got older, he became less dependent (and less interested) in these frequent FaceTime calls—eventually answering "uh huh" to most of her questions. Now when she is away and she FaceTimes her son, they chat a bit and then just leave the camera and sound on while they work and do homework—giving them each the feeling they are in the same room.

Mindy Simon also uses technology to be in the same room with her children—even helping her kids practice the piano over FaceTime. "You don't have to physically be there to be *there*."

Know there's room in your schedule for school events that matter most.

As a former C-suite executive, Sharon Callahan-Miller's schedule was jam-packed. She was also a single mother, so she felt supporting her family meant she couldn't go to every event at her sons' schools. Though she felt justified, she also felt disconnected whenever she couldn't attend and worried she was letting her sons down.

A colleague told her to reframe the dilemma. "If you had a toothache, you would always find time to go to the dentist. We assume we have no room in our schedule, but in reality, things can always be moved around to accommodate events important to our kids."

From that point on, Sharon rarely missed a baseball game or special event. "Know which events really matter to your kids and be there for those. You don't have to attend absolutely everything. And make sure your assistant is a good gatekeeper who keeps the blocks of time you need to be out of the office off-limits."

Chapter 19

Expand Your Definition of Family Time

- Start the day on the right foot.
- Give your family confidence they have your undivided attention.
- Normalize the professional work you have to do at home.
- Live in the moment—at work and at home.
- Reevaluate what's *really* important to your children.
- Free up your weekends for more fun.
- But don't make weekends the end-all, be-all.
- Ask for help with the hard stuff so you can focus on what's enjoyable.
- Emphasize everyday things you can do easily as a family.
- Find lifelong memories in the special and the mundane.
- Take a day off to be with your children after a busy period at work.
- Spend special alone time with each of your children.
- Keep the element of surprise.
- Find creative ways to connect with your kids.
- Create sacred family time through shared passions.
- Bond with your children by bonding with the world.

WHAT WILL YOUR KIDS REMEMBER about the time you've spent as a family? It's the big things, like trips to exciting places and the smaller but still significant traditions, like baking holiday cookies.

In this chapter you'll see memories are made from both the magical and the mundane. The message that came through loud and clear from the women I spoke with: make the time you spend with family simply about being together. It doesn't always have to be a big event that takes lots of planning. These women have been mindful about creating blocks of time their children can count on, but they also fill mere minutes with routines that have a lasting impact.

Start the day on the right foot.

Working mothers aren't the only ones who have busy schedules... both parents and school-age children leave in different directions for days that are equally jam-packed.

To make sure everyone was grounded at the beginning of each day, BET Networks Chief Marketing Officer Kimberly Paige made a hot family breakfast. This not only provided a healthy meal, but it also nourished her family's communication.

"You can cover a lot of important ground in the conversations you have before your family scatters every morning at 7:30."

After breakfast, Kimberly drove her children to school, always with the same parting words: to her daughter she said, "Show them how beautiful, smart, and kind you are," and to her son, "Show them how handsome, smart, and kind you are."

Give your family confidence they have your undivided attention.

Janet Foutty has always considered family time nonnegotiable. When her children were young, her phone stayed in her work bag until they were in bed. After that she would pick up with work when necessary.

Before she retired, she often had her phone on airplane mode on weekends, so she wouldn't be interrupted. At work she was fully on, and at home she was fully off—a discipline she attributes to simple pragmatism. "I knew my organization was working on incredibly important initiatives... but they were not life or death. A call could always be returned an hour or two later."

Karen Jones also came to the conclusion that a job doesn't make the world turn. Earlier in her career she was glued to her BlackBerry—she was a true "CrackBerry" addict with fear of missing out on real-time email activity. She found herself looking at her device throughout dinner and at other times she should have been present for her family.

Knowing she had to stop the distraction—and addiction—she decided to go cold turkey. She finally put her BlackBerry away during all family times... and usually discovered later that nothing critical had happened requiring hypervigilance.

Normalize the professional work you have to do at home.

Bath & Body Works President Julie Rosen made sure she was home to have an early family dinner at least three or four nights a week. Then there was always a family dinner on Sunday, so everyone would start the week together.

During the workweek, after dinner dishes were cleared, everyone knew Julie needed to sign back on to her computer.

"No one thought it was unusual for me to do more work after dinner. My sons had homework to do after dinner, too."

Live in the moment—at work and at home.

Mindy Simon is realistic about the times she needs to be a Chief Operating Officer at home and a mom at work. Things are going to escalate, at times, on either side.

She knew she had to leave the office the day her mother said, "Your father didn't get out of bed today," because her sixth sense had been telling her he was in his final decline. And there are times when she's home and a work project suddenly goes downhill, and she knows her team needs to go to the office.

"Be in the moment and do what's urgent even if you're supposed to be on work or home time. Explain to your kids that it goes in both directions and it all evens out."

Reevaluate what's *really* important to your children.

While Shannon Lapierre was growing up, her thrifty mother always sent her off to school with a brown bag lunch. Shannon always wanted the hot lunch (which at the time seemed like the cool option), so she was happy to give her own daughter money to buy lunch at school.

One day her daughter was very upset and said she wanted her mother to make her lunch every day. "All the kids who have stay-at-home moms have really interesting, healthy lunches."

On Sundays, Shannon and her daughter would then plan and make lunches together and box everything up for the week.

Free up your weekends for more fun.

In the early years of your career, it can be expensive to outsource household responsibilities. But even when your paycheck may be smaller, Martha Leiper, Unum's Chief Investment Officer, recommends a housekeeper once a week.

"Don't spend your precious family weekend time doing tedious housework. Your children will not remember your house was spotless—they'll remember they had fun with you."

But don't make the weekends the end-all, be-all.

Everyone looks forward to the weekends, but it's impossible to fit in everything a family wants to do in 48 hours. Sometimes all the hype for the weekend falls flat.

To take the pressure off "the perfect weekend," Martha Leiper designates Wednesdays as family nights. "We'll see a movie or go out for a casual dinner, so we've already done something special in the middle of the week."

Ask for help with the hard stuff so you can focus on what's enjoyable.

One beauty industry Chief Executive Officer trained herself to ask for help so she would have more time for fun. When her son was a toddler, she always raced home in time to give him a bath and put him in his pajamas. After a long day at the office, she had the often-stressful task of wrangling an unwilling toddler into the bathtub.

She soon realized that a simple change—asking their caregiver to handle bath time—would give her the time to play games and read books before bedtime, which was a more low-key and joyful way to spend time together.

"I recognize how lucky I am. Not everyone has a full-time, in-home caregiver, but there is probably someone you can ask for even occasional help. You don't have to do everything on your own."

Emphasize everyday things you can do easily as a family.

A trip to the beach or the museum takes some planning, and with family members going in many different directions it might not be possible to do these things very often.

To more regularly spend time as a family, Sharon Ryan made cooking dinner most nights a family endeavor. Everyone in her family loves to cook, and it's a time to come together and talk casually.

Sharon also dubs herself the "craft queen"—she always brought home projects they could do together, like buying cement to make hand imprints, making a doll, or tie-dyeing a blanket.

"These are the things my daughters remember—not that I took business trips to China for 10 days."

Find lifelong memories in the special and the mundane.

Jill Timm and her husband have taken their family on many trips they will always remember as cherished family time. But they also preserved Sundays as the time when they were all always home. Any work or errands Jill needed to do never happened on Sunday. Her girls could depend on that day as time when they all didn't do anything necessarily special...but they were together.

Take a day off to be with your children after a busy period at work.

When Shannon Lapierre would be head down at work for a few weeks, she would then take a Friday off and give her daughter an afternoon off from school. On this day they would play hooky, go out to lunch, do something fun together—always a special time to reconnect and make up for the fact she had been consumed by work for a period of time.

Spend special alone time with each of your children.

Time spent together as a family is important, but Jordana Kammerud also makes a point of spending time alone with each of her two children.

"The amount of time you spend with each child matters less if you have special alone time. It can be an hour I spend just talking with my son or a fun afternoon activity with my daughter. Anything that shows

I'm fully focused on and interested in what they're thinking, feeling, and doing."

Keep the element of surprise.

As it is with all families, Julie Rosen and her children had predictable daily routines. One of the ways she showed each of her sons she was not all work and no play was a once-a-year surprise hooky day—a time when mother and son got away from their usual commitments.

On the designated hooky day, each son could choose what he wanted to do—and have a fun day alone with his mother. They could go to a museum, the aquarium, out to lunch—whatever they chose.

"Kids often think their working parents do nothing but work. I'm always thinking of ways to inject our routines with unpredictable and unplanned fun."

Find creative ways to connect with your kids.

Many mothers get one-word answers to the question "How was school?" Especially as kids get older, they tend to clam up about their days.

Jennifer Piepszak has a work-around for kids who are not big communicators: focus on special interests you can share.

Like her sons, Jennifer has always liked sports and keeps ESPN on her Instagram feed. "There's always something to talk about that my sons find very cool conversation—what this team or that player is doing. It's not as exciting to talk about math or gym class."

Create sacred family time through shared passions.

Though Nora Zimmett's television news career keeps her away from home until 9:00 p.m. during the week, she doesn't worry about time away from her daughter. She knows they spend big chunks of time together on the weekends pursuing their shared passion for horseback riding.

Nora grew up riding horses and passed on this interest to her daughter. Initially her daughter was fearful, but over time it became a wonderful way to instill confidence in a sport—and in life. Now her daughter is an avid equestrian, competing in horse shows that are often miles away.

"Nothing makes you closer than a five-hour car ride to an activity you both love. The time away creates the opportunity for long conversations that show me who she is as a person...not just a kid who needs her homework checked."

Bond with your children by bonding with the world.

Homework, meals, bath time, errands, chores, carpooling. Days whiz by in a blur—filled with many routine tasks. Any time we spend with our children is good time, but Joy Corso considers the most special bonding when you work together to help others.

Joy joined the National Charity League—an organization that provides volunteer opportunities for mothers and daughters. Each month she and her daughter attend meetings and choose projects they'd like to do together.

"These activities get us out of school, work, and household routines and spark great conversations about how to help people in need. Around the holidays we visit nursing homes and bring Christmas cards and cookies. During short volunteer stints we learn more about each other and become more grounded in the world that surrounds us."

Chapter 20

Find Room in Work and Life
for Aging Parent Needs

- Look for early signs your parents or in-laws will need financial help.
- Know the cost of eldercare.
- Give aging parents the gift of your time.
- Realize you can't fix everything for an ailing parent.
- Separate your feelings from aging parent needs.
- Use your business acumen to help aging parents decide where to live.
- Avoid the fight with fiercely independent aging parents.
- Make one sibling CEO of eldercare.
- Look beyond gender and proximity when assigning family eldercare responsibilities.
- Give siblings very specific eldercare jobs.
- Be the primary caregiver's emotional support.
- Keep all family members in the loop.
- Realize you can find work that has room for eldercare.

THE YEARS YOU SPEND CARING for your young children are both wonderful and stressful. Then when your children are almost grown and flown, your fourth job begins... caring for aging parents and in-laws. In my opinion (after overseeing care for my father and in-laws), the cost, stress, and unpredictability of eldercare can be more challenging than raising a child.

Women are most often the caregivers for aging parents (59 percent), and on average the time they spend is at least 20 hours of unpaid work. On top of that, many of these caregivers have paid jobs and they're also raising children. The burden of multi-generational caregiving often leads women to cut back on their paid work hours or leave the workforce entirely.[1]

At quick glance, these statistics may seem to apply only to women providing hands-on care for aging parents. Women who oversee care also spend many hours a week on endless logistics. Both my husband and I were working full time when my mother-in-law had 24-hour care that still required our constant attention.

Unlike a child, though, elderly parents are in the last chapter of their lives. You're acutely aware that time with them is short, and you want to be with them as much as possible. Though many women interrupt their careers to care for children and then later for parents, few of the executives I spoke with left their jobs. Instead, as they also recommend for the child-rearing years, they have had open conversations with their boss and found ways to work flexibly during the challenging eldercare phase.

Look for early signs your parents or in-laws will need financial help.

Not all aging parents are forthcoming about their personal finances. What their adult children may not know? Twenty percent of adults age 50 and older have no retirement savings, and 61 percent worry they won't have enough money to support themselves in retirement.[2]

This dire news impacts adult children trying to save for their own retirements.

There are certainly many cases when financial difficulty is obvious, but if your parents generally seem okay financially—or even in the more affluent category—you might not know if they could potentially outlive their money.

Dana White's father had a good job as a civil engineer, but the Senior Managing Director of the Global Strategic Advisory Practice at Ankura Consulting Group (formerly Chief Communications Officer at Hyundai Motor North America) could see from an early age he had challenges managing and saving money. Her mother worked a series of less lucrative jobs that allowed her to prioritize her children. Together, her parents put their children's needs ahead of their own financial future. After her father died, she thought about the fact her maternal great-grandmother lived to age 100, and it was not unusual for the women in her family to live well into their 80s and 90s. She knew her mother would likely need to fund a long life, too.

Early on in her career Dana faced the realities of her parents' financial situation, asked the questions she needed to ask, and began planning for eldercare alongside her own retirement. "I was motivated by the fact that financial security for me (as a single woman) and my mother relied on my ability to succeed. I have two wonderful brothers, but I knew they would have financial responsibility for their own families. I'm grateful my work has afforded me the resources to provide a level of financial security that eluded my mother most of her adult life."

Know the cost of eldercare.

Few people investigate the cost of eldercare until a parent has an urgent need. They don't know what the costs are for home care or in a facility— nor have they figured out how long their parents' nest egg will actually last.

Even once-affluent parents who reach their 90s could outlive their money, which is not hard to imagine when you consider these median eldercare costs in the United States[3]:

- Assisted living in a group residential setting: $4,995 per month
- 24/7 memory care in residential facility: $6,200 per month
- In-home care: $30 per hour (or $21,600 per month for 24/7 care)

"Women have to think ahead, run the numbers, and plan for their own healthcare and overall retirement needs—and also factor in the potential needs of parents and in-laws," says Sharon Ryan. "This is all the more reason to work consistently. I was grateful for my uninterrupted earnings when we first had a caregiver come to my dad's home—and the price tag was $30,000 per month."

Karen Jones agrees that the astronomical cost of eldercare really hits home when it is multiplied by four—potentially covering both parents and in-laws. She has always known her father does not have enough savings to cover eldercare and sees her ongoing work as a way to support her extended family.

Give aging parents the gift of your time.

Just before Jill Penrose reached the officer level, her mother had stage 4 breast cancer. It was a difficult 10-month period, and her mother lived nearly four hours away.

At a critical point in her career, Jill was anxious about being away from the office. She put her fears aside and arranged an intermittent leave—a reduced schedule that included two days working in the office and one day working at her mother's home.

"I was grateful to be able to take this time and proud that when I returned to work full time, I transitioned successfully. Shortly after returning I received a promotion I had worked hard to achieve. This was an empowering lesson for me: you are viewed in a long lens as a professional and you don't need to sacrifice the time your family needs you because you will still progress in your career."

Realize you can't fix everything for an ailing parent.

As a very organized and busy person watching her elderly mother decline over four years, Anne Foulkes felt she had to step in and fix everything she possibly could. During that difficult time when her mother was still living independently and experiencing the first stages of dementia, she would call Anne 20 times a day. It was very disruptive, but Anne was terrified not to answer.

Eventually the problem of her mother living precariously at home alone was solved by settling her into a local retirement facility. But even in this setting, Anne had to realize she couldn't—and shouldn't—fix every problem that arose.

One issue: when her mother thought people were stealing her belongings. Rather than fighting a losing battle to convince her mother she was wrong and get the staff involved, she let minor problems go. This reduced Anne's stress and gave her the chance to inject a little more lightheartedness into their relationship. Knowing her mother loved chocolate, for example, Anne kept her nightstand full of cookies and chocolate bars.

"There are so many things out of your control. In non-life-threatening situations, take off your executive hat, give yourself a break, and think of simple things that bring happiness and comfort."

Separate your feelings from aging parent needs.

Decisions are never easy in eldercare situations. When it came time for her father-in-law to enter a care facility, Suzanne Powers was a sounding board and support for her husband and his family as they all approached the situation with facts, analysis, and research.

"I see it as similar to selecting a vendor in business. We took the emotion out of it and considered it a project. We can feel what we want, and there are plenty of emotions all the way around. But truth, facts, and evidence tell us what we need to do."

Use your business acumen to help aging parents decide where to live.

Chandra Dhandapani's aging mom is in her eighties and living thousands of miles away in India. She shares responsibility for arranging caregiving with siblings and has also learned to take the emotion out of conversations about whether her mother should move to assisted living. Instead, like Suzanne, she assesses the situation as she would a business issue.

"What's the context of the problem and my mother's real motivation for wanting a certain situation? What is my mother trying to accomplish? What is she telling me or not telling me? Rather than just saying, 'This is best for you and we're going to make the decision for you,' we come at it from a much more thoughtful and informed place."

Avoid the fight with fiercely independent aging parents.

Shannon Lapierre's aging parents would allow very little outside help and did not want to burden their adult children. Not abiding by their wishes led to arguments, so she found ways to help without taking away their independence.

Shannon recognized getting out and about was still important to her father, for example, so she hired a companion just to take him on errands, instead of much dreaded full-time care.

And rather than telling her parents she was making meals for them she would sneak things in during her visits with a simple, "Oh, I made too much dinner last night and brought you some of the extras."

Make one sibling CEO of eldercare.

For two years Dana White lived in California while her mother lived in Virginia—and although her two brothers live within driving distance to her mother, it was always assumed that Dana would take the lead on her eldercare needs.

In so many families, siblings have difficulty sharing the responsibility for aging parents—and when everyone is in charge no one is in charge. Ultimately, it leads to a lot of family strife. Dana advises families to decide early on who will take the lead, and then divvy up responsibilities from there.

"In my family we decided that even though I'm the youngest, I'm basically the family CEO. It has worked well for us—it's easier for my mother to speak primarily to me about her needs."

Look beyond gender and proximity when assigning family eldercare responsibilities.

Marie Robinson knows care for aging parents can sneak up on you and disrupt all your best-laid career plans.

Her father went into the hospital for heart surgery, and that unexpectedly triggered an extreme decline into dementia. After he passed away, she and her siblings needed to see her mother through the loss of her husband and make sure her mother's trust and estate planning was complete.

At first, as the eldest, the only daughter, and the one who lived closest to her mother, Marie shouldered all her mother's needs. She soon realized she needed to be vulnerable and ask her two brothers for help. Now they all share responsibilities for her mother's care and estate planning, and they have regular Zoom calls to keep each other up to date.

Give siblings very specific eldercare jobs.

When parents start to decline, adult children often have trouble keeping responsibilities equitable and organized. Inevitably, one or two siblings feel they are doing everything, or multiple siblings get little done trying to take care of the same tasks.

Unum Chief Investment Officer Martha Leiper was living in Texas when her mother was suffering from Alzheimer's in Tennessee. She has 11 siblings, which could have turned into chaotic caregiving. Instead, certain siblings took the lead on their mother's care—each with specific jobs. Martha handled finances, another was in charge of medical bills, and others who lived nearby shared doctor visits.

"When a parent is ailing, there can be a free-floating feeling when you're not sure what to do. Assigning very specific responsibilities gives siblings more structure and the ability to maintain their own goals and independence when the family's world seems upside down."

Be the primary caregiver's emotional support.

When Allstate Chief Legal Officer Christine DeBiase's mother was battling cancer, she and her family made the decision to move their mom from her home in New Jersey to live with her sister, Linda, in Texas, who had a flexible job. Although Christine and her other sister, Maria, visited often, Linda was the daughter who was the primary caregiver and carried great responsibility every day.

"The best way we could support Linda as she tirelessly cared for our mother was to be her emotional support. We were the outlet for her to express her fears and frustrations and we checked in with her often, so she knew we were always present despite the distance in miles."

Keep all family members in the loop.

Former Deere & Company General Counsel Mary Jones has family spread across the world. Her aging parents live close to her and her sister (who also has a professional career), and their brother lives in Norway.

To make sure everyone is in the loop about the needs of their parents, the three siblings share information through regular group texts or emails. "We don't want any out of sight, out of mind situations. We all know who is taking the lead on an issue, but we can also offer suggestions or just generally express appreciation and support. And it's also a way for everyone to know how much needs to be done, and when it makes sense to rebalance responsibilities."

Realize you can find work that has room for eldercare.

When Dana White realized her mother needed hands-on care, she made the difficult decision to leave her job as the Chief Communications Officer for Hyundai. While she loved that high-profile job, she knew she had to give more time to her mother. She was confident this decision would not be the end of her career: she has had many exciting roles through the years, including working for a United States president, two senators, two four-star generals, and the CEOs of three global Fortune 500 companies.

Dana also knew how she felt when she was working in Paris and her brother called her with the news that their dad had died alone. "I was heartbroken. Even though my mother said we all take birth and death journeys alone, I still struggle with the fact that I wasn't there in the days before he passed. I will never be cavalier about proximity to my family again."

"When it came time to leave Hyundai, all my colleagues were extraordinarily supportive. They offered me a sabbatical and supported remote work from my mother's home in Virginia, but for the first time in my life I decided to prioritize family over work. So I left and took the time and space necessary to focus solely on my mom. It was a good decision, because she spent the next two months in the hospital."

"I later had a conversation with the CEO of Ankura, my current employer, and I shared the situation I had with my mother. Without skipping a beat, he said, 'Live where you want and do whatever you need to do.' I was so grateful for his trust and confidence."

Chapter 21

Volunteer with Passion and Precision

- Volunteer to help others—and yourself.
- Find volunteer roles that have a simple playbook.
- Get involved at school when you're not involved at work.
- Bring your management skills to school.
- Be the school volunteer your child can see.
- Volunteer selectively—and follow a passion.
- Donate your time to support your kids' interests.
- Share school volunteer jobs with your spouse or partner.

IN REALITY, VOLUNTEERING COULD BE a fifth job. But the executive women I spoke with have found ways to make a significant contribution to schools and community organizations without putting in too many hours.

Yet again, women use their business skills to make their volunteer hours more efficient and impactful. They have fewer weekday hours to contribute to great causes, so they find things they can do at night or on the weekends. And they take the lead in spreading the work among more volunteers.

In most cases, executive women favor school volunteer roles when their children are young. Nothing makes a child happier than seeing their moms at school, and even the visibility from a few volunteer projects a year goes a long way.

Volunteer to help others—and yourself.

Volunteering may require less time and have more benefits than you think.

As a busy executive, Chandra Dhandapani has been wary of volunteer roles that would require too much time. But through a role limited in scope and predictable for her schedule, she learned that volunteering not only gives you the opportunity to give back and make a difference... it also gives you new perspectives you can apply to work.

Chandra serves on the board of trustees for her son's school—a volunteer role that sounds demanding and complex, but actually is contained within a few meetings a year. The headmaster of this school for boys always says the work of the board should be driven by how they want the boys to feel: they should feel known and part of a community where people care about them and everyone is invested in their success.

Realizing this mission applies to her work environment as well, Chandra made a conscious effort to be less clinical and transactional and lead with humanity. "Now I start conversations at work with a sincere and personal question about how each person is doing in all aspects of life." This more personal check-in deepens her professional relationships and enhances collaborations with colleagues—giving them a stronger foundation to solve problems.

Find volunteer roles that have a simple playbook.

Mary Mack also knew she didn't have a lot of time to volunteer—or the creativity to be the room mother leading craft projects. Her answer was to become a Junior Achievement classroom volunteer—taking advantage of an "off-the-shelf" lesson plan and limited advance preparation.

It worked out for everyone: her six-times-a-year visits to the classroom were firmly in her calendar, she got the face time she wanted with her daughters and their classmates, and she could be back to work the same day. This volunteer role also gave her a way to manage her daughters' expectations; they knew exactly when they could count on her to be at school.

Get involved at school when you're not involved at work.

It's not easy for working mothers to go on field trips or work in the school library during the workday. But the answer doesn't have to be no involvement at all.

Martha Leiper signed on to volunteer at times that would not conflict with her work schedule. She accompanied the football team while they helped out at a homeless shelter on Saturdays, became the head timer for weekend swim meets, and capitalized on her business connections by making fundraising calls in the evenings.

Similarly, Raj Seshadri found volunteer jobs that could be done at night and on weekends. She took the job of organizing the sports team parents, for example—figuring out who would bring snacks when—because she could do all the scheduling when she had free time.

Bring your management skills to school.

Though Kris Malkoski initially felt she didn't have the time for any significant school volunteer activity, she knew it was the best way to stay on top of what was happening socially and academically. She dove in and became head of the PTO not once, but three times. She didn't allow endless talk about what kind of flowers to have at events—everyone knew she would stick to an agenda and start/end meetings on time.

Like she did for her household, Kris created factbooks for each PTO committee so chairs would have all the information they needed and cut down on unnecessary phone calls and emails. Each factbook included the purpose of the committee, the role of each committee member, contact information for key teachers and administrators, key dates for events, and timelines for development/planning.

"A very high level of business organization allowed me to volunteer at the same or even a greater level than mothers who did not work professionally."

Because she is also hyper-organized, Anne White was able to find time to be a room parent—a job not often sought after by those who work full time professionally. Rather than thinking she had to handle every last detail, however, her team management approach got more parents than usual involved.

"Spread the responsibility over several people, and schedule activities far in advance, and you'll make it possible for more working mothers to be involved."

Be the school volunteer your child can see.

When one beauty industry Chief Executive Officer was growing up, her mother was an active volunteer—but it was often behind the scenes. Knowing young children love to see their mothers at school, this CEO chooses to volunteer when it involves interacting with her son.

"All volunteer jobs are important, and I'm so grateful for time each parent contributes. I've found if I can volunteer in person—or my son can participate in a volunteer project at home (picking out decorations for class parties, for example)—I get the double benefit of helping the school and spending time with my son. It's important to show him we are both part of the school community."

Sharon Ryan and her husband tried not to miss a school event or opportunity to volunteer in the classroom while her daughters were young. "This is the time when your kids are so proud to have you at their school. As they get older, it doesn't matter to them as much."

Volunteer selectively—and follow a passion.

Busy women barely have time to do everything they need to do for their homes and their families. Requests for their time as volunteers comes from all directions—for schools, sports teams, religious groups, community organizations, and more. Women feel obligated to contribute their time to further good causes, but the hour here and there can add up and cause more life stress.

Joy Corso admits she's not a big "get involved" person. But when she found a cause that was personal to her, she said it was easier to find the time. Before her nephew passed away, he had wished for a big baseball scoreboard in his hometown. The Make-A-Wish Foundation awarded him the gift posthumously. That led Joy to approach their local chapter and ask to serve on the board.

Now an active board member, Joy says, "It's not really a time commitment, an obligation, or another job. It's a contribution to something that my nephew ignited in my heart."

Donate your time to support your kids' interests.

Despite busy work schedules, Mary Jones was always an active volunteer—for organizations aligned with her kids' interests.

One big example is serving on the board of a local summer camp. "I looked for opportunities to show my kids I was working to make something they cherished—like summer camp—even better. And I always wanted them to appreciate the need to be involved in the community."

Share school volunteer jobs with your spouse or partner.

Jill Timm has had a creative approach to school volunteer roles—she shares them with her husband. Through the years they have capitalized on their finance expertise and served as co-treasurers of the PTA and the Parent Athletic Association.

"This gave us both the opportunity to be involved—and we switched off on the meetings to accommodate our busy schedules."

Chapter 22

Reconsider Turning Down
the Next Big Role

- Don't assume you can't handle a big promotion.
- Avoid catching imposter syndrome.
- Be vocal about what would make you say yes to a promotion.
- Put guardrails around a decision to stay put.

ALL C-SUITE WOMEN INTERVIEWED FOR this book were at the career crossroad of "Should I or shouldn't I take that promotion?" at least once. With 4 Jobs, they had biting-off-more-than-you-can-chew trepidation.

In most cases they forged ahead, putting trust in company leaders who trusted they could do the job. They asked a lot of questions, accepted there would be a learning curve, and asked colleagues for help.

Sometimes, though, women knew the timing was off. In these situations, they didn't say "never"; they said "not now." They made it clear they were open to a promotion in a certain amount of time.

Honest conversations with your boss and your family keep your career moving whether you choose a straight or more circuitous path. My coaching clients often surprise themselves: they're much more ready for a promotion than they anticipated, or with careful work–life strategy they circle back to bigger opportunities sooner than planned.

Don't assume you can't handle a big promotion.

Lots of women tell Anne White they're fine in their current position... because they don't want to rock the boat and take on that next big responsibility. "But I tell them to think of their careers as a series of steps, not leaps."

When women say they could never head a business unit as she does, she points out they will not necessarily work more hours than they do now. "Each step you take prepares you for the next big challenge. Don't self-select out. When you're at higher levels of leadership you have more control of your time, and you have the chance to delegate more. It's a process... you don't have to rise to CEO tomorrow."

Jennifer Piepszak also believes promotions are not as monumental as many women fear. "When you start a new job there's a learning curve, maybe more intense work for a bit—but it quickly normalizes. It's the early years when you actually do the hardest work."

Avoid catching imposter syndrome.

Tonit Calaway knows women often suffer from imposter syndrome and a lack of confidence. (That's why a former Wall Street CEO once told me every single man on her team marched into her office to ask for a raise... and every woman did not.)

If you have a good relationship with your boss, Tonit says, trust their instincts about whether you're ready to handle the next step in your career. When she told a woman on her team she was being promoted to Vice President, the woman said she wasn't sure she wanted to take the opportunity. Specifically, she wasn't sure she could handle the extra work when she also had so many responsibilities at home.

Tonit told this woman that her promotion was a bit of a formality—because she was already doing the level of work required for the VP job. Tonit then said, "Are you saying you don't want the title and extra money?" (Upon further reflection, the woman took the title, the money, and the job and continued to manage work and life just fine.)

Jennifer Piepszak says it's the imposter syndrome—not necessarily the bigger title—exerting more stress on your work and life. Especially when women think they must be the smartest person in the room.

"You don't want to be the smartest in the room; you want to be the person everyone wants in the room. Someone they can trust and the one who is a great problem solver, asks the right questions, works collaboratively, is fun to be with, and visibly enjoys both work and life."

Be vocal about what would make you say yes to a promotion.

When Mary Jones had young children, her company sent many people on expat assignments. There was a general perception you had to accept one of these assignments to advance your career.

Living in another country was a nonstarter for Mary's family, but she made it known she'd be willing instead to do extended business travel. She described the kind of assignments she would welcome. At the time, the company was building their office of compliance, and she traveled around the globe with the head of this division. Her husband, an electrical engineer, worked close to home. He developed a local clientele to minimize his travel and was able to do a lot of the caregiving when she was away.

"If you're proactive, you can put yourself in the position to pick and choose the big responsibilities that fit your life."

Put guardrails around a decision to stay put.

If you don't have the bandwidth to reach for that next big opportunity now, but you want to leave the door open for the future, Jacinth Smiley suggests making it clear your current decision could change. Give an initial timeframe—say, for example, you'd like to stay in your current role for the next one to two years. Agree to discuss your work–life situation every six months or so.

"In the meantime, strive to be a pillar of the organization. Continue to grow through your depth of expertise and experience. Recognize that every organization needs these critical pillars as bench strength."

Chapter 23

Be a Work–Life Leader

- Show your humanity.
- Spread the work to build leaders and reduce stress.
- Support or start parent and caregiver employee resource groups.
- Declare No-Meeting Fridays!
- Help your boss be more empathetic.
- Be the change you want to see.

ONE OF THE BIG REASONS I wrote this book relates to a data point in a national survey I conducted: *Women in 2020: Choosing to Move Up the Career Ladder—Or Not?*[1] At the time, I found that only 57 percent of mid- to senior-level women felt women in power were doing enough to model ways of blending work and life.

This survey was conducted before the pandemic, and my discussions for this book show the sea change of support now found at the senior level. But there's always more to be done, and it's not only up to senior leaders.

Anyone, at any level, can be a leader, especially when it comes to being vocal about work–life issues. Speak up and suggest useful programming for your women's and parenting employee resource groups. Think

through how everyone on your team (both male and female, both parents and non-parents, people involved in eldercare) could benefit from
more flexible work arrangements. Collaborate closely with colleagues so
more projects can be shared. Think, generally, of finding solutions for all
the people who share the common goal of blending work and life.

Show your humanity.

Jennifer Piepszak had a deal with her three sons: "No matter what, you
can always reach me."

She once left a meeting when her college freshman son called. What
he did he want? The one-time passcode for Amazon.

Jennifer likes to tell stories like this, so she is relatable to colleagues
and to younger women in the thick of work and motherhood. Another
great example: during the pandemic everyone in her family was working under one roof, and she felt it was important for one son to do his
schoolwork in their home's designated office. She was then relegated to
the laundry room—where she situated herself so the washer and dryer
were not visible during Zoom calls. But she told everyone anyway the
laundry room was her command central.

Former Voya Investment Management Chief Executive Officer Christine Hurtsellers also believes managers at all levels can teach healthy
work–life habits by example. Once she was leading a conference in Boston with hundreds of people who had flown in for the event. In the middle of her remarks, she got a call from her special needs son who was
having a meltdown.

The evening had just begun, and Christine was supposed to lead
more discussions and join the group for dinner. She stayed true to her
"family first" mantra, she told the crowd "the wheels are falling off the
Hurtsellers bus," and she left the event.

"Leaders have to lead in both work and life. Both women and
men need to see that it's okay—and expected—to put family first. I
told my son he could always reach me, and I would always be there for

him—regardless of the situation. That's a promise I will always very visibly keep."

Spread the work to build leaders and reduce stress.

Leadership is leveraging the strengths of those around you so the whole team performs at peak efficiency without individual burnout. Today there is leadership in promoting work–life collaboration.

In Anne White's view, "Delegating often gives others a growth opportunity, and gets you out of the trap of thinking you need to do everything. Teach the benefits of delegating and collaborating all the way down the line."

Anne gives lots of projects to her EA, for example, that other EAs wouldn't typically do. This frees up some of Anne's time, but it also gives her EA a much more interesting job description—which is probably why she has stayed in the job for more than 10 years. "You don't always have to be the one giving the speech or going to the meeting. The more the whole team gets involved, the less stress on one individual person."

Support or start parent and caregiver employee resource groups.

Mary Jones was the executive sponsor of the Deere Parents and Caregivers Connection—one of many employee resource groups at the company.

"Finding the right caregiving for children or aging parents can be difficult. In Deere's ERG [employee resource group] we've shared ideas and resources and talked about what is and is not working for our families. Representatives of local facilities have also been invited—so employees can see the breadth of resources in our area."

Aditi Javeri Gokhale has a similar role as the executive sponsor of Northwestern Mutual's Women's Initiative and also the African American Employee Resource Group. To make it successful and meaningful, she says, "Make your group part of your company DNA… not just a 'project' for a group of mid-level employees. Make sure you get buy-in and dollars from the top as well as allies throughout the organization."

Declare No-Meeting Fridays!

Karen Jones has often been pulled in a million directions at work. To gain more control of her time (in an environment when someone wants a meeting every hour of every day), she declared No-Meeting Fridays.

"I will, of course, meet with my boss if necessary—but to everyone else my calendar is off limits. Friday is my day to catch up on everything, write a presentation, clear out emails—and feel organized and ready for the next week."

Help your boss be more empathetic.

In the line of fire, company leaders can be fully distracted by the work at hand. Despite this, Penny Pennington says you should not be afraid to speak up and talk about work accommodations for a life challenge you're facing or some kind of work flexibility you need as you're raising your family.

"It's not that company leaders aren't human, it's that they're consumed by work. And sometimes male leaders need a few more reminders that we all have 360-degree lives."

Penny told a story about a female executive who was discussing all that needed to be organized at home before she traveled to an off-site meeting. She then turned to a male colleague and asked, "Do you have to do all those things before you travel, too?" He did not, and it was a reminder to be more cognizant of the added responsibilities women face at home.

Be the change you want to see.

"We are they" was the mantra Janet Foutty had while she was rising in her career. She didn't join in when her colleagues complained that "they" (senior management) were rigid in continuing with "the way things have always been done." Instead, she always said that as a team we should create the kind of environment we *all* want to work in...one that ultimately is palatable for everyone and maintains peak productivity.

As a young mid-level professional, Janet worked hard to promote flexibility and predictability for all members of her team—at all levels. She was not the boss, but she knew she could still make suggestions and influence office culture. Ultimately, she was able to create a schedule mothers could count on for their childcare needs—consistently working late only on certain nights, for example. The culture she promoted on that long-ago client team made it possible for 10 mothers to continue working and reach the partner level.

Chapter 24

Seize Opportunities for New Work and Life Chapters

- Consider reinvention at any age.
- Take advantage of natural career breaks when you can.
- Be open to where a family-driven career change may lead.

W E ALL KNOW LIFE HAS many twists and turns. The process of writing and publishing a book is long, and during the many months this book was in development, about one third of the women moved on from the company they worked for at the time they were interviewed.

Some women decided it was time to retire, others pursued opportunities at new companies, and a few totally changed careers. Conversations with these women show their willingness to branch out, take risks, and continually open new and interesting doors at every age and life stage. In today's world "retirement" is indeed a dated concept and "work" over the span of a lifetime can take many forms.

A Bureau of Labor Statistics study that followed baby boomers from age 18 to 56 found that women have held an average of 12.5 jobs over their lifetime—suggesting both optional and forced reinvention.[1]

Perhaps the best advice of all is to keep your eyes wide open and always know your options. Change can be welcome or unwelcome, and at each life stage you need to be ready to act on challenges and opportunities. As reinvention guru Lesley Jane Seymour (now the founder of CoveyClub, an online and in-person community that helps midlife women figure out what's next and the former Editor in Chief of the first magazine focused on reinvention, *More*) says, "Always have a reinvention plan in your back pocket."

Lesley advises with pragmatism: "You'll be forced to reinvent at some point. It's not an if, it's a when. A change can be driven by health, relocation, divorce, job loss, an empty nest, or just plain boredom." She notes, "No career is a straight shot anymore—many millennials in their 40s have already had close to a dozen jobs." In the volatile magazine industry, Lesley had seven jobs, and she counts her current entrepreneurial venture as her eighth.

Most of all, when it comes to your career, Lesley says, "It ain't over until you say it's over." Her CoveyClub membership has an average age of 54, and she has seen women make huge leaps into an entirely different field—like one who left finance and became a pediatrician. Or many who make less dramatic changes, moving from one side of a business to the other.

The two things reinventors need to become comfortable with, according to Lesley, are risk and fear. Throughout this book you've heard about women who have never been afraid to pivot. They slowed down a bit and took on different roles when they needed to spend more time with family. They moved from big-name corporations to lesser-known boutique firms. Morphed from advertising executive to executive coach. Took sabbaticals and traded global posts for jobs close to childhood homes. Capitalized on many years in corporate America and launched their own start-ups. Developed expertise in a low-key government job until the time was right to take on the big-law-firm partnership track. Switched careers and industries: private equity to Pitney Bowes; digital marketing to insurance; technology to management consulting; jewelry to glass manufacturing.

And through every chapter they found hundreds of simple ways to manage four big work and life jobs with sanity, good humor, and grace.

Consider reinvention at any age.

Sharon Callahan-Miller never thought her career would have a hard stop at the traditional retirement age of 65.

At age 59, after nearly four decades in the advertising industry, she started thinking about possible new chapters. As a CEO, she experienced the challenges and triumphs of leading an organization. After 12 years, she realized her ability to cultivate people and shape careers could have an even bigger impact. Though she loved her time in advertising, she felt increasingly restless and eager to go off on her own.

"My age was never a factor because there's still so much more I'd like to experience professionally. Entrepreneurial ventures have always intrigued me, and I realized my true calling, at this stage of my life and career, is guiding and empowering other leaders to reach their full potential. Through executive coaching, I leverage my own senior-level experiences to mentor and inspire others, helping them navigate the complexities of leadership and achieve their professional and personal goals. Now I have the platform to make a meaningful impact on a broader scale and contribute to the development of strong, visionary leaders in not just advertising, but many industries."

Take advantage of natural career breaks when you can.

Before her post at Stanley Black & Decker, when Shannon Lapierre was working as Chief Communications Officer at The Hartford (a big insurance company), there was a restructuring that created a natural exit. Rather than jump right into her next role, she decided to take a break. For the next 18 months, she spent time with her teenage daughter, took care of her aging dad, and hit the gym.

She also pursued a master's in communications, finally earning the advanced degree she had always wanted.

"This was one of the best periods of my life. From college on, I was always focused on rising in my career, going from next, to next, to next, often working under a high degree of stress at companies undergoing major crises. This career break was about me and my family. I spent quality time with my daughter, truly getting to be part of her daily life; got back in shape; and continued my education. It seemed like such a risky career decision, but it has had such a lasting, positive impact."

Fast-forward nearly nine years: now Shannon is on her second career sabbatical after six-plus years as head of communications at Stanley Black & Decker.

"This was another point when I could have rushed into another role. But I learned some valuable lessons from my last career sabbatical. My work tends to require an all-in approach, and the time between jobs allows me to regroup, reprioritize, and learn, which makes me a better leader and better person. Once again, it feels like a very risky career decision, but with confidence and faith you can expect the right path to appear at the right time. Recognize that time is a gift."

Be open to where a family-driven career change may lead.

Though Ankura Consulting Group Senior Managing Director of the Global Strategic Advisory Practice Dana White has technically been her mother's caregiver since 2011, there were periods when they lived many miles apart.

At different times in Dana's career, her mother lived with her in Virginia. Then the opportunity to be the Chief Communications Officer for Hyundai brought her to the West Coast, and her mother was stable enough for Dana to make the move.

This situation changed after her mother fell twice and never regained mobility. Dana knew she was needed back in Virginia, but, as mentioned earlier, it was also difficult to leave her job at Hyundai.

Initially, Dana was concerned she wouldn't find a role as interesting or lucrative as the one she left behind. She decided to broaden her search into management consulting, knowing her many government and corporate experiences gave her broad perspectives to advise clients. She ultimately got a new job that has taken her in many new directions—focusing globally on technology consulting and the amazing new world of AI.

As it has turned out, Dana's move back to Virginia brought several silver linings: special time with her mother, learning a new industry, broadening her portfolio of skills—and a very flexible employer who makes it possible to manage multiple work and life roles as her mother's needs ebb and flow.

ENDNOTES

Introduction

1. "Labor Force Status of Women and Men," US Department of Labor, dol.gov /agencies/wb/data/widget, March 2024, accessed July 4, 2024.
2. Caroline Fairchild, "Nearly Half of Mothers Work, Take a Break, and Work Again. Why Is There Still Such a Stigma?" LinkedIn, linkedin.com/pulse /nearly-half-mothers-work-take-break-again-why-still-stigma-fairchild/, March 4, 2020.
3. "Breaking Boundaries: Women Poised for Milestone Achievement in Otherwise Bleak Outlook," S&P Global Market Intelligence, spglobal.com/esg/insights /featured/special-editorial/breaking-boundaries-women-poised-for-milestone -achievement-in-parity-amid-otherwise-bleak-outlook, August 2023.
4. Kathryn Sollmann, *Ambition Redefined: Why the Corner Office Doesn't Work for Every Woman & What to Do Instead* (Boston and London: Nicholas Brealey Publishing, 2018).

Chapter 2

1. Elizabeth J. Altman and Beth K. Humbard, "The Gendered Division of Household Labor and Emerging Technologies: The Promise of Artificial Intelligence and Autonomous Vehicles," brookings.edu/articles/the-gendered -division-of-household-labor-and-emerging-technologies/, September 2023.
2. Eve Rodsky, *Fair Play: A Game-Changing Solution for When You Have Too Much to Do and More Life to Live* (New York: G.P. Putnam's Sons, 2019).

Chapter 4

1. "Labor Force Status of Women and Men," US Department of Labor, dol.gov /agencies/wb/data/widget, March 2024, accessed July 4, 2024.
2. Kara Baskin, "Working Moms Are Mostly Thriving Again. Can We Finally Achieve Gender Parity?" Working Knowledge, Harvard Business School, https://hbswk.hbs.edu/item/working-moms-are-mostly-thriving-again

-can-we-finally-achieve-gender-parity#:~:text=Can%20We%20Finally%20
Achieve%20Gender%20Parity%3F,-by%20Kara%20Baskin&text=The%20
pandemic%20didn't%20destroy,Kathleen%20McGinn%20and%20Alexandra
%20Feldberg. September 14, 2023, accessed July 4, 2024.

Chapter 5

1. Jena McGregor, "Companies With Flexible Work Policies Outperform on Revenue Growth: Report," Forbes, November 14, 2023, https://www.forbes .com/sites/jenamcgregor/2023/11/14/companies-with-flexible-remote-work -policies-outperform-on-revenue-growth-report/, accessed July 4, 2024.
2. "The Flex Report," Flex Index, Scoop, www.canva.com/design/DAGERvg IWLI/FoyrKrZxYPbQpYyGTdI7wA/view?utm_content=DAGERvgIWLI& utm_campaign=designshare&utm_medium=link&utm_source=publish sharelink, accessed July 4, 2024, Quarter 2, 2024.

Chapter 6

1. "Motherly's 2024 State of Motherhood Report," Motherly, https://www .mother.ly/news/2024-state-of-motherhood-report/, accessed July 4, 2024.
2. Michael Madowitz, Alex Rowell and Katie Hamm, "Calculating the Hidden Cost of Interrupting a Career for Child Care," Center for American Progress, Cap 20, https://www.americanprogress.org/article/calculating-the-hidden -cost-of-interrupting-a-career-for-child-care/, June 21, 2016, accessed July 4, 2024.
3. "This Is How Much Child Care Costs In 2024," 2024 Cost of Care Report, Care.com, https://www.care.com/c/how-much-does-child-care-cost/, accessed July 4, 2024.

Chapter 7

1. "Women@Work 2024: A Global Outlook," Deloitte, https://www.deloitte .com/global/en/issues/work/content/women-at-work-global-outlook.html, accessed July 4, 2024.

Chapter 8

1. "Women in the Workplace Study: The State of Women in Corporate America," Lean In, https://leanin.org/women-in-the-workplace?gad_source=1&gclid=Cjw

KCAjwkJm0BhBxEiwAwT1AXNWgDlYRSFHUTn0tt4_I3GQQ_K5w0fDhVm
R0zCs50cltW4h9eZEQJxoCvVYQAvD_BwE, accessed July 4, 2024.

2. "Caregiver Statistics: Work and Caregiving," Family Caregiver Alliance,
caregiver.org/resource/caregiver-statistics-work-and-caregiving/, accessed July 4,
2024.

3. Kathryn Sollmann, *Ambition Redefined: Why the Corner Office Doesn't Work for Every Woman & What to Do Instead* (Boston and London: Nicholas Brealey Publishing, 2018).

Chapter 10

1. Linda Babcock and Sara Laschever, *Women Don't Ask: Negotiation and the Gender Divide* (Princeton, NJ: Princeton University Press, 2021).

Chapter 11

1. Megan Leonhardt, "Childcare, Housekeeper, and a Personal Assistant: Women Are Paying Big Bucks for Support at Home in Order to Reach the C-Suite," yahoo! finance, https://finance.yahoo.com/news/steep-cost-success-female-executives-171212607.html?guccounter=1&guce_referrer=aHR0cHM6Ly93d3cuZ29v Z2xlLmNvbS88&guce_referrer_sig=AQAAAAFFNXnIXBf4ET-9ga0HoLK KxF4VGzStnz5gRnW2yKb5p-Q8UPtQJCLHgp1gubvgqt5Ha_4AbplovcFSn4 RuReq8zc8UNMzECozbpQ6xQraFgVbQzZg6xymxM8inOonYTQU0RxVR _xrHqh00cav_mGdFsudyEt6PvE_Q71l0QeaL, accessed July 4, 2024.

Chapter 12

1. Julie Lythcott Haims, *How to Raise an Adult: Break Free of the Overparenting Trap and Prepare Your Kid for Success* (New York: Henry Holt and Co., 2015), p. 200.

2. Eve Rodsky, *Fair Play: A Game-Changing Solution for When You Have Too Much to Do and More Life to Live* (New York: G.P. Putnam's Sons, 2019). *More Life to Live*, p 7.

Chapter 13

1. Lynn Okura, "What Is Perfectionism Really Hiding?", HuffPost, https://www.huffpost.com/entry/brene-brown-perfectionism-shame-oprah_n _4045358, October 5, 2013, accessed July 4, 2024.

2. Laura Vanderkam, "Time Strategy #4: Satisfice," Habits, lauravanderkam .com, lauravanderkam.com/2016/07/time-strategy-4-satisfice/, July 22, 2016, accessed July 4, 2024.

Chapter 14

1. "Motherly's 2024 State of Motherhood Report," Motherly, https://www .mother.ly/news/2024-state-of-motherhood-report/, accessed July 4, 2024.

Chapter 15

1. Kenneth R. Ginsburg, MD, MS Ed, FAAP, Ilana Ginsburg, and Talia Ginsburg, *Raising Kids to Thrive: Balancing Love with Expectations and Protection with Trust* (Itasca, IL: American Academy of Pediatrics, 2015), p. xv.

Chapter 20

1. Sarah House, Shannon Seery Grein, Nicole Cervi and Aubrey George, "Can't Grow Old Without Her: Women's Central Role in a Growing Eldercare Economy," Wells Fargo Economics, https://wellsfargo.bluematrix.com /links2/html/d9b56735-644a-42af-a714-8919998a0470, accessed July 4, 2024.
2. "New AARP Survey: 1 in 5 Americans Ages 50+ Have No Retirement Savings and Over Half Worry They Will Not Have Enough to Last In Retirement," https://press.aarp.org/2024-4-24-New-AARP-Survey-1-in-5-Americans -Ages-50-Have-No-Retirement-Savings#:~:text=WASHINGTON%E2%80 %94A%20new%20AARP%20survey,to%20support%20them%20in%20 retirement. April 24, 2024, accessed July 4, 2024.
3. "2024 Report: Cost of Long-Term Care and Senior Living," A Place for Mom, https://www.aplaceformom.com/senior-living-data/long-term-care-costs.

Chapter 23

1. Kathryn Sollmann, "Women in 2020: Choosing to Move Up the Career Ladder—Or Not?" https://www.linkedin.com/in/kathrynsollmann/details /featured/.

Chapter 24

1. "Number of Jobs, Labor Market Experience, Marital Status and Health for those Born 1957–1964," US Bureau of Labor Statistics, August 22, 2023, bls .gov/news.release/nlsoy.nr0.htm, accessed July 4, 2024.

ABOUT THE AUTHOR

Kathryn Sollmann encourages women to *always work* in some flexible way from college to retirement.

Throughout her career she has found creative ways to manage 4 Jobs—professional roles, alongside raising two daughters (now 33 and 24, living in New York City and pursuing their own careers), caring for aging parents and managing a busy household.

Harder than any professional job, Kathryn says finding and keeping great childcare was the most challenging part of working motherhood. She tamped down guilt about not being with her children 24/7 and hired many great live-in and live-out nannies (ranging in age from 20 to 60) for the toddler years, and high school students when her daughters needed only after-school care.

Running the household is a responsibility she has always shared equally with her husband, also their chief gardener. An avid cookbook reader, she does all grocery shopping and cooking. Housecleaning is #9,000 on the list of things they want to do, so early on they made room in their budget to outsource that task. They've found an easy rhythm for all other household needs—alternating who makes the calls for repairs, who takes out the garbage, and who makes the bed. Most of all, they enjoy decorating their 1938 home.

When it comes to self-care, Kathryn is religious about a Pilates class at least four times a week. She loves to knit, needlepoint, read and entertain family and friends.

Even when her daughters were quite young, Kathryn's family traveled frequently—and they still explore many corners of the world together, including recent safaris in South Africa and Zimbabwe. They also return frequently to Nantucket where it is a tradition to spend time with extended family.

Kathryn has worked non-stop in many ways—first in traditional corporate roles, and then finding more flexibility by launching several entrepreneurial ventures, advising investment clients as a marketing consultant, and helping current and returning professional women navigate careers. *The 4 Jobs Club* is her second book. She has no plans to ever retire.

Since the days when everyone was tied to their desks, Kathryn has always found ways to work—and be an involved mother. She drove thousands of carpooling miles, did many tours as room mother, planned fundraising events and brought snacks to sports games where she cheered on her daughters.

Family has always been first, but everyone knows that work is part of Kathryn's DNA. When her children needed her less and aging parents needed her more, she took on the eldercare job driving to doctor's appointments, managing hospital visits, overseeing moves to assisted living, arranging a revolving door of caretakers and walking on eggshells when proud but ailing parents actually did not want the help.

Kathryn empowers women to build their own financial security. Always building the community of smart women helping other smart women, she provides the tools and strategies to manage the 4 big jobs that fund and provide fulfillment in an interested and interesting life.

ACKNOWLEDGMENTS

A true partner in work and life, my husband of nearly 40 years, Rob Soll-mann, has given me limitless encouragement and support for this book and the many chapters of my career. He has not only inspired me and our two daughters to reach for our stars, but also helped many women advance in the workforce throughout his long and successful executive career.

My generous and always loyal sister-in-law, a fellow writer, Ryder Wyatt, has cheered me on through my first and second books—and I have appreciated all the wisdom she has shared from her own valuable instincts and her vast community of prominent authors.

After writing my first book, I thought I had checked a big goal off my bucket list and that it was "one and done." Thanks to my friend, the Tony Award–winning producer and playwright Tracey Knight Narang, who scoffed at that notion and got my wheels turning for this book with a simple "I think you have another book in you."

Indeed I did, and I wrote this book to help women navigate their 4 Jobs and find many practical ways to stay in the workforce for long-term financial security. My dear friend, the age-defying Ginny Corsi, who worked well past the traditional retirement age creating synergy for many businesses and executive teams, has always been a shining example of a very full life well lived.

And finally, a huge thank-you to my wonderful agent, Linda Konner, who brought my career full circle. After college, I wanted a publishing job, but the prospects were slim during an economic downturn. In the category of "it's never too late"—and after an eclectic career that has spanned the investment world, career coaching, communications, marketing, event planning, executive recruiting, and corporate training—I'm here, finally, with two books in the publishing world, helping women find the work that fits their lives.